THE LETTERS OF SIGMUND FREUD
AND ARNOLD ZWEIG

L. G. Hawkins

Cambridge, June 1971

THE
LETTERS
OF
SIGMUND FREUD
AND
ARNOLD ZWEIG

Edited by
ERNST L. FREUD

Translated by Elaine and William Robson-Scott

A HARVEST BOOK
A HELEN AND KURT WOLFF BOOK
HARCOURT BRACE JOVANOVICH, INC.
NEW YORK

ISBN 0-15-650680-7

Library of Congress Catalog Card Number: 74-95859

Printed in the United States of America

A B C D E F G H I J

ACKNOWLEDGEMENT

Permission to publish Letters Nos. 230, 255, 257, 264, 276, 278, 285 of *The Letters of Sigmund Freud*, Selected and Edited by Ernst L. Freud, © 1960 by Sigmund Freud Copyrights Ltd, London, Basic Books, Inc., Publishers, New York, was kindly granted by Basic Books, Inc.

EDITOR'S FOREWORD

THE plan to publish the following correspondence dates back to the year 1955, when Arnold Zweig placed copies of Freud's letters to him at the disposal of Ernest Jones for his biography of my father. From that date Zweig never ceased to hope that these letters might appear in book form. It was not, however, until 1963 that he asked me to act as editor and at the same time to arrange for an English translation.

Even after Zweig had removed a few of the more personal passages from his letters, certain further cuts still seemed desirable to me: on the one hand some too detailed accounts by Zweig of his neurosis and analysis, and on the other hand all too frequent and exaggerated eulogies of my father. All these omissions were carried out in agreement with Dr. Adam Zweig of Basel, who had been entrusted by his father with this task.

The German edition of the correspondence appeared in 1968, published by the S. Fischer Verlag, Frankfort, only a few months before Zweig's death, and I hope he was still able to enjoy the great interest it evoked among the reading public and the praise accorded it by the critics.

As editor I should like to thank the translators, Professor and Mrs. W. D. Robson-Scott, and also the English and American publishers, The Hogarth Press and Mr. Masud Khan, editor of the International Psycho-Analytical Library, and Mrs. Helen Wolff of Harcourt, Brace and World, New York, respectively.

London, March 1969   ERNST L. FREUD

NOTE ON ARNOLD ZWEIG

ARNOLD ZWEIG was born in 1887 at Glogau, Silesia, the son of a saddler. Gifted with an exceptional mind, he studied history, philosophy, and literature at various German universities. In 1913 he made his first mark in literature, with the novel *Novellen um Claudia* (translated into English as *Claudia*).

When World War I broke out, Zweig, like so many of his contemporaries, volunteered for army service and fought as a private in France, Hungary, and Serbia. He left the army a confirmed pacifist. The novel that established his international fame, *The Case of Sergeant Grischa* (1927), is based on his own combat experiences. It was the first of a cycle of war novels, among them *Education Before Verdun* (1935).

In 1933 Zweig emigrated via France to Palestine. He returned to his native East Germany in 1948, following an invitation of the East German government. There he was made president of the East German Academy of Arts and awarded the Lenin Peace Prize from the Soviet Union for his series of anti-war novels. He died in East Berlin, almost totally blind, in 1968.

CONTENTS

THE LETTERS OF SIGMUND FREUD
AND ARNOLD ZWEIG

Dear Professor Freud,

May I make a request of you? I would like to have your permission to dedicate my book *Caliban oder Politik und Leidenschaft, Versuch über die menschlichen Gruppenaffekte, dargestellt am Antisemitismus*[1] to you.

My gratitude to you has many aspects and it is this that moves me to make my request. Firstly, because without your system of thought, your basic ideas and your new principles (the reintroduction of the psyche into psychology), without your creative philosophic method my own modest contribution to theoretic knowledge would never have been possible. Secondly, because anti-semitism, which you must have experienced in all its aspects, owes you an obeisance. And thirdly, because I personally owe to your psychological therapy the restoration of my whole personality, the discovery that I was suffering from a neurosis and finally the curing of this neurosis by your method of treatment.

I still cherish the hope of being able to make your personal acquaintance. I think I could supply you with a number of significant insights into neurotic inhibitions affecting the creative artist which might perhaps confirm certain observations made by you long ago.

Today I only hope that you will agree to accept the dedication of a book which you do not as yet know, but which owes so much to you. In any case I remain always

Your faithful admirer

Arnold Zweig

[1] Gustav Kiepenheuer Verlag, Potsdam, 1927.

Dear Sir,

I accept with thanks and a full appreciation of the honour done me the offer of the author of the *Novellen um Claudia*[1] to dedicate one of his new works to me.

This I would have done in any case, and now my pleasure in accepting is all the greater on learning from your letter that you have a true appreciation and personal experience of analysis.

Please fulfil your promise to visit me one day. (Don't wait too long, I shall soon be 71.)

Yours very sincerely

Freud

Vienna IX, Berggasse 19
2 June 1927

Dear Sir,

Caliban arrived here today. The book shall accompany me on my summer holiday to the Semmering (2½ hours' journey from Vienna), when I go there in a fortnight's time. There I shall read it and if anything worth while occurs to me I will write and tell you. But don't count on this; my horizon is narrow, and I do not easily find my way in territory where I am not at home. Also I've got all kinds of uncharitable prejudices with regard to humanity. But why should I forestall your critics!

Kindest greetings and thank you once again for the contact which your book has established between us.

Yours

Freud

[1] English translation: *Claudia*, Viking, New York, 1930; Martin Secker, London, 1930.

Vienna IX, Berggasse 19
2. xii. 27

Dear Dr. Zweig,

Many thanks for sending me your new book,[1] which I very much look forward to reading. I read your *Caliban* during the holidays with great interest, partly with warm agreement and partly with critical reserve. I was very proud of the message you dedicated to me, but then again annoyed that you made an obeisance to Karl Kraus[2] who stands at the very bottom of my ladder of esteem. In so far as I was put off by anything in the book the fault no doubt was mine. With regard to anti-semitism I don't really want to search for explanations; I feel a strong inclination to surrender to my affects in this matter and find myself confirmed in my wholly non-scientific belief that mankind on the average and taken by and large are a wretched lot. Naturally I am not reproaching you with having managed not to surrender to this irrational affect. I did once go into the 'differential feelings' of which you speak. I spoke about a narcissism of the minor differences.[3] There is much about them that remains enigmatic.

Eichkamp
18. 2. 29

Dear Professor Freud,

I would have liked very much to have a word with you in Berlin, but I knew that you were unwell and I did not wish to intrude upon the rest you needed. I am not even sure whether I sent you my *Sergeant Grischa* or whether

---

[1] English translation: *The Case of Sergeant Grischa*. Viking, New York, 1927; Martin Secker, London, 1928; also Hutchinson International Authors, 1947.

[2] Karl Kraus (1874–1936): Satirical writer; editor of *Die Fackel*.

[3] S. Freud: 'The Taboo of Virginity'. *Standard Edition of the Complete Psychological Works of Sigmund Freud* (hereafter abbreviated *St. Ed.*), XI, pp. 191 ff.

3

Pont und Anna[1] has reached you, both books which I would rather think of in your hands than in anyone else's. Perhaps your daughter[2] could send me a line about this, so that any omission may be made good.

Today I am really writing to explain the enclosed letter from Einstein. From the short résumé, which I would earnestly ask you either to read for yourself or have read to you, it emerges that since we have no state of our own and since the states in which we live are fully occupied providing as well as they can for their own artists, we are anxious to help—in the first instance in Berlin and then later in other centres of Jewish intellectual life—those of our creative artists who are completely without any organisation to support them here in Western Europe. They find themselves in this position, because they belong either to the exiled sections of the Russian bourgeoisie and write in Russian, or because they come from Poland and the Ukraine and write in Yiddish, or because they came over from Palestine and write in Hebrew. In addition to these writers, scholars and poets there are a number of artists and journalists and a few German poets of Jewish extraction who because of various inhibitions and peculiarities find it impossible to make a living, even though they are men of talent. As I have always taken up the cause of German intellectual workers, I know how hard it is to secure any public funds even for them. We just manage to keep them from starving. But for these Jewish intellectual workers, and especially for those among them who do not write in German, there exists no single body, no single state and no single charitable organisation which can relieve us of our responsibility towards them. Since we cannot permit them to perish among us here in silence and since the need is far too great for any single Maecenas to bring more than temporary alleviation to a few, we have decided

[1] A. Zweig: *Pont und Anna*. Gustav Kiepenheuer Verlag, Potsdam, 1928.
[2] Anna Freud, born 1895, Freud's youngest daughter.

to set up from our own resources the organisation which is described in the circular enclosed. Our sole request to you, Professor Freud, is that we might add your name to our honorary committee. You will be kept informed of what is happening, and no further claims will be made upon you, beyond asking you to lend the weight of your name to a cause for whose existence the need is urgent.

If we succeed in getting the matter going in Berlin, and the auspices for our success there are good, since we have already secured the disinterested support of men of means and of business ability, the organisation will be extended to include Austria, the C.S.R.[1] and Poland, where the need is just as great as in Berlin itself.

I trust that I shall not have asked in vain, and I think we shall soon be able to provide you with further clear evidence of the seriousness of our intent and the efficiency with which we are carrying out the work. Meanwhile I shall conclude with the expression of my gratitude and regard.

Yours sincerely

A. Z.

Vienna IX, Berggasse 19
20. ii. 29

Dear Sir,

Let me deal first with personal matters. I did receive a copy of *Sergeant Grischa* from you some time ago. I like the book very much and I seldom miss an opportunity of praising it. I do not as yet know *Pont und Anna,* and if you don't send me a copy soon I shall have to buy one myself. I heard somewhere that these 2 volumes are part of a trilogy and that the last volume has not yet appeared. I'm not trying to retaliate when I ask if you already possess a copy of my last little book, *Die Zukunft einer Illusion.*[2] I shall probably not

---

[1] C.S.R. = Czechoslovak Republic.
[2] S. Freud: *The Future of an Illusion. St. Ed.* XXI, pp. 5 ff.

publish anything further unless I am definitely pressed to do so.

On March 11th I hope to be in Berlin-Tegel again (sanatorium).[1] Perhaps for one or two weeks only, but it would be very nice if I could see you. My son, Ernst Freud,[2] lives at Regentenstr. 23. The organisation you are endeavouring to establish naturally has all my sympathy. Although I haven't much else to give, I feel almost hurt that you should ask me to give only my name. How often do I not envy Einstein the youth and energy which enable him to support so many causes with such vigour. I am not only old, feeble and tired, but I am also burdened with heavy financial obligations. I should like to become a subscribing member of your society, but the main thing is that you should find numerous better members than me. In the cultural institutions with which I am connected – the Psychoanalytic Press, the Teaching Institute, etc. – I am confronted daily with the misery of insufficient financial support and the indifference of the wealthy classes. And in the first place I must be a psychoanalyst and fulfil my destiny.

Hoping to hear from you and to see you soon.

With kind regards
Yours
Freud

Eichkamp
5 March 29

Dear Professor Freud,

You will receive in due course a formal expression of our thanks for your kind words and for your decision to join our committee. But today I would like to answer personally and

---

[1] The first psychoanalytic clinic, directed by Dr. Ernst Simmel, who put his house at Freud's disposal during his stay in Berlin.

[2] Ernst Freud, born 1892, Freud's youngest son.

6

tell you how much I (and my wife) are looking forward to meeting you. I do not know whether I told you when I wrote to you about *Caliban* that were it not for analysis I should never have regained access to my creative faculties and that your great discoveries and your methods have made me what I am today. But I will tell you more about that when we meet—such things must be told, not written. *Pont und Anna* contains in very disguised form an abbreviated narrative of this matter. But later and on a large scale I would like to give an outline of the cultural development of man or at any rate of Western man by means of a description of the development and cure of two cases of neurosis. I only wish that I could soon start on this novel which shall be central to my work.

Pont und Anna was really written *before Sergeant Grischa* and was published in 1925, but the general public wasn't interested in the book *Regenbogen*[1] where it appeared. Now people's eyes are naturally open to it, but it is wrongly interpreted as being one of the sequels of the *Sergeant*. But you know the Europeans; there's no need for me to waste any more words on that topic.

I read *The Future of an Illusion* in proof, and was enchanted and stimulated to contradict. For I have naturally devoted much thought and intuition to this matter, and thanks to the analytic method, *your* method, I have made some discoveries which I would like to set out in an essay on the Divine. But I would first like to tell you my thoughts on the subject.

In the meantime kind regards, in which my wife also joins.

Yours gratefully
Arnold Zweig

[1] *Auswahlreihe des Volksverbandes der Bücherfreunde*. J. M. Späth Verlag, Berlin, 1925.

Dear Professor Freud,

The doctors say that I must take care of my eyes, but what point would there be in that, if I couldn't write to you personally to say how my heart was warmed by the good town of Frankfort bestowing upon you the Goethe Prize. For pleasure in someone else's success is the finest pleasure there is, and you too must surely have felt some pleasure about this and perhaps have felt also that your deep pessimism about the future of analysis is not quite justified after all. This Goethe Prize has not been tarnished by being bestowed too lightly; without overestimating Stefan George, he is certainly a man who has never compromised; Albert Schweitzer is an almost overwhelming figure in this day and age (do you know anything about him?) and now you—the most upright, the most fearless standard-bearer for the use of human reason. The town of Frankfort is to be congratulated! For you we wish a peaceful holiday on the Grundlsee after your exhausting time in Berlin,[1] and may you be able to enjoy the evening sunshine there. With warmest greetings to your family, and especially to Fräulein Anna.

Ever yours
Arnold Zweig

Grundlsee
21. 8. 1930

Dear Dr. Zweig,

Of the many congratulations which the Goethe Prize brought me none has touched me so deeply as the one which you extorted from your poor eyes (though there is no evidence of this in your handwriting) and this is obviously

[1] Reference to Freud's stay in Berlin to be treated by Prof. Schröder prior to the making of a new prosthesis for his jaw.

because I feel with you as with scarcely anyone else that my friendship meets with a real response. I do not deny that I was pleased about the Goethe prize. The thought of a closer connection with Goethe is very tempting, and the prize itself is more an act of deference to the person than an appraisal of his achievement. On the other hand, at my time of life such recognition has neither much practical value nor great emotional significance. For a reconciliation with my contemporaries it comes pretty late and I have never doubted that long after my day analysis will finally win through. As I read your letter I discovered that I would have been not much less pleased had they given you the prize, and it would really have been more appropriate. But no doubt many similar things lie in store for you.

My wife and daughter send warm regards to you, and to your wife whom I would like to thank especially for her congratulations. My daughter will represent me at the Goethe celebrations in Frankfort.

With every good wish

Yours

Freud

Leermoos

Drei Mohren

8. 9. 30

Dear Mr. Freud,

This removal of your title is the immediate result of your bestowal upon me of the rank of doctor–something which I would sooner receive at your hand than at anyone else's, but to which I am not by right entitled. For I never considered myself capable of gaining an academic degree, very erroneously as I now see, and so I must spend the rest of my life naked and exposed, just a simple man in my own name. This is a deprivation under which I suffer particularly when I remember the present state of our universities.

Your letter, your dear long letter, written in your own hand brought me, along with everything else, one great joy—for the scepticism about the future of analysis stems not from me, dear Mr. Freud, but from you. You alarmed me with it during our conversation in your flat in Vienna, among all the treasures and sacred objects which the tombs have had to yield up to you who have opened up so many a tomb. You then uttered bitter words of deep disappointment and I recall precisely the arguments with which I countered yours, though I had little confidence in their efficacy, when they were set against the feeling that you, the creator, had about your own creation. I am now happy to learn that your low opinion of the worlds of today and tomorrow was to be attributed more to a passing gloom in your feelings than to a Freudian judgement. No one is more entitled to feel this gloom than you, but we are delighted to see it dispersed, and not least for your own sake, for those of us who have experience of analysis have no doubt as to its indestructibility. We are only sorry that you do not feel that so vital, dynamic and revolutionary an intellectual principle as yours, once launched upon the world, will continue to be effective until it has finally overcome all the blunt resistance the world can offer.

And now about writing in one's own hand—naturally I like writing to you in the same way as you do to me and I don't like letting a machine intervene in our warm personal contact with one another. But I am obliged to go warily in this, for the scar on my left eye, to which I paid no attention, has now been there for five years and the eye has still not reached the point of allowing me to work as much as I would like to. But now my right eye is playing a trick on me which I cannot conceal from you as a psychologist. I must tell you that in the act of seeing a small bubble of liquid is produced in the retina, as in a camera, so that in the centre of my field of vision I see a dim round gluten, which is more or less opaque, surrounded by a dark ring. This ring acts as a kind of framework, and circumscribes the area on which the bubble touches the retina. Now ever since mid-May on this central area, which is of a greyish yellow brightness, grimacing faces have been appearing. They appear both by day and by night, literally at every moment, both when my eyes are closed and when they are open. These faces change more or less according to the rhythm of my pulse beats; they take on different shapes, but they are always some variation on the face of a man with a moustache. During the first few months they were Jewish faces. My eye conjured up every type of Jewish face for me. Then later they were mainly faces of recumbent men, seen from the chin upwards, their eyes shut, and so the faces of dead men. Some days they changed into decomposing, disintegrating faces, then again into death's heads, often too into something like portraits of intellectuals wearing the clothes of remote centuries, complete with skull-cap and pointed beard. On one solitary occasion this optical camera produced for me a female face; once again it was dead and decaying, with a short nose and a sort of crown above its brow.

You can imagine how these phenomena have irritated, but at the same time interested me. During an excursion here I made the acquaintance of a Viennese neurologist, Dr. Sch. by name, as I sat next to him all day in the car. Towards the end of our acquaintance I told him about this phenomenon out of curiosity to hear what he would say. But he thought that I had possibly seen it once involuntarily and that now I expected it to recur, so that in this way I personally contributed to its reappearance. Naturally I was forearmed against such an argument. I know how a man behaves when he is entirely passive and never for a moment remotely imagines that he is going to see, let us say, a death mask of Frederick II against the background of a forest, compared with a man who is nervous and who says to himself 'Will that optical illusion occur again now?' and who conjures it up for himself in this way. The phenomenon has the stability of a hallucination, but is considerably less strong, and it is restricted to the production of a characteristic male face, either dead or alive, drawn in dark lines upon a yellowish background. I can tell you right away that my own explanation of this optical illusion is based, or two-thirds of it at any rate, on the man in the moon. The drop of liquid on my retina sets up irritations in the optical nerve underneath and this latter reacts by producing alternations of light and shade, since this is the only way it is able to respond. Human imagination imposes images of organic nature wherever it is possible, on clouds and mountains and preeminently on faces, and so my imagination produces this ceaselessly changing man in the moon who corresponds to recent incidents in my intellectual life with which my imagination is concerned. For when someone recently read aloud to me Malraux's unusually striking book *The Conquerors*[1] to distract me a little from my own concerns, the face repeatedly assumed a Chinese aspect. Malraux's story takes place in Canton in 1925 and is just the sort of book that would make an impression on one's imagination. And yet, as I said, this explanation is only two-thirds satisfactory to me. I will not say yet what the other third consists of, as I'm not yet sure of it, but it is highly likely that behind these repeated dead faces lie feelings of guilt towards my father and my father-in-law; unresolved associations, which I want to examine analytically before reporting further on them. The Jewish faces were replaced by other more general types when I went more deeply into the problem of the Jew and Jesus in writing my new novel[2]–a kind of self-analysis, if I might call it thus, which uncovered a whole series of not uninteresting, ambivalent nodal points.

To quote Goethe, I can see how broad and long[3] I have grown and I hasten to conclude.

[1] André Malraux: *Les Conquérants*, 1927.
[2] English translation: *De Vriendt Goes Home*. Wm. Heinemann, 1937.
[3] Cp. *Faust*, Part 1, l. 1250.

It is certainly satisfactory to be able to lock up the Frankfort document in one's desk, but if you want to have a good
laugh at one of the articles churned out by the Jubilee I will
send you an essay from the *Vossische Zeitung*, written by a
doctor who to my great delight defends the Soul and
Experience against analysis. Unfortunately he has got less
of an idea about analysis than I have of aviation, though
you will agree with me that even about aviation only the
man who has had long experience of flying has any idea, and
better still if he has piloted the plane himself.

This time it is glorious in Austria. I am brown and happy,
and my wife too is in comparatively good health (the
altitude here did not suit her in bad weather). And I have
finished a little surprise for you here, which I hope to send
you by the end of the month. I won't say any more about it
now except that there are few readers to whom it will appear
so crystal clear throughout as to you.

And with that, I wish you an Indian summer as glorious
as Stifter[1] made it, and I am delighted to sign myself

As ever

Yours

Arnold Zweig

Kind greetings of course to your good daughter and to your
wife.

Grundlsee
10. ix. 30

Dear Arnold Zweig,

I hasten to confess to you how ashamed I am of my mistake. I had a feeling of uncertainty, it's true, as I wrote
that title down, but since there were obviously unknown
forces involved it is not surprising that I quickly silenced
those warnings. The analysis I immediately carried out on

---

[1] Adalbert Stifter (1805–68): Austrian writer. The reference is to his
famous novel, *Der Nachsommer*, publ. 1857.

this *Fehlleistung* [slip] of mine naturally led on to delicate ground; it revealed as the disturbing factor the other Zweig, whom I knew to be engaged at this moment in Hamburg in working me into an essay[1] which is to bring me into public notice alongside Mesmer and Mary Baker Eddy. During the last six months he has given me great cause for annoyance; my original strong desire for vengeance has now been completely banished into the unconscious, and so it is quite possible that I wanted to make a comparison and establish a compensation.

I only know Dr. Sch. by name. I know that he belongs to the school of Wagner-Jauregg[2] and I am not at all sorry that you should have encountered in him an example of official clinical acumen. In contrast to this, I regard your non-doctrinal explanation as correct in all three thirds. The indefiniteness of the sensory perceptions stimulates the central tendency to create illusions, which are then elaborated by unconscious phantasy. The situation appears similar to that prevailing in so-called 'crystal gazing', concerning which Silberer[3] published some remarkable observations in an early volume of our journals. I am sorry that I am far from my library at the moment. Oddly enough pictures of old Jews were prominent there too. Your experience with the Chinese faces is certainly a decisive proof and your suspicion about the old men in your family is highly probable. It may also be assumed that one's own personal expectations of death provide the driving force. The whole phenomenon will probably disappear one day, and were it not so tormenting it would provide an excellent opportunity for self-analysis. Through the gap in the retina one could see deep into the unconscious.

[1] Stefan Zweig (1881–1942): *Die Heilung durch den Geist.* Insel Verlag, Leipzig, 1931. English translation: *The Mental Healers.*

[2] Julius von Wagner-Jauregg (1857–1940): Prof. of Psychiatry, Vienna. Awarded Nobel Prize 1927.

[3] Dr. Herbert Silberer, member of the Vienna Psychoanalytical Society.

I was not aware of any contradiction between what I said when you visited me and what I wrote in my last letter, nor of any change in my expectations as a result of receiving the Goethe Prize. It is easy for me to say this, because I have absolutely no idea what I said to you then. Forgetfulness about one's own remarks is indeed particularly strong and alleviates all manner of contradictions. What is interesting at the moment is the attitude of my contemporaries, who are already seeking to compensate themselves for the honour they were forced to pay me in Frankfort. The news is going round in a number of German and foreign newspapers that I am hopelessly ill with cancer of the tongue. As a result of this I am now receiving as many messages of condolence and suggestions for treatment as I received congratulations last week! It is amazing how many absolutely reliable cures there are for this disease.

With warmest greetings to you and your wife

Yours
Freud

Berlin-Grunewald
16. 9. 30

Dear Mr. Freud,

Again and again you surprise and shame a younger man with the speed, the thoroughness and the kindly sympathy with which you answer my communications, which can form after all nothing but marginal notes to your daily intellectual activity.

It is nice to be corroborated and at the same time so outstripped by you in the understanding of a condition into which you have only been able to peer through an imperfect medium. Certainly I must have an intensive preoccupation with death—at the moment I will not venture to say more than that. For example, while I was in Leermoos writing my

15

letter to you I received an invitation from the *Weltbühne*[1] to write something for their 25th jubilee. What was the first thing that occurred to me? To make a survey of all the dead people who as critics and thinkers had been important literary examples to me, who had been my intellectual fathers, so to speak. I summoned them up very exactly, from Poppenberg to Jacobsohn with characteristic epithets, before adding my congratulations to the still extant *Weltbühne*.

My heart, which the doctors say is quite sound, has indeed been giving me more trouble at this altitude of 1000 m.–in depressive weather, it's true–than one bargains for on a holiday, and I am somewhat puzzled what to do. Self-analysis would be fine, were it not that the wonderful precision with which you dissect your *Fehlleistung* [slip] did not prove to me something that I know already: namely that my analyst Dr. K. is a splendid and excellent fellow, it's true, but he has not learnt how to perceive carefully nor to classify all the minute details which must be taken into account if one is going to interpret a phenomenon really thoroughly. And since I cannot work more exactly than I have been taught, at least not on and by myself, this self-analysis will perhaps be limited to disentangling a few important individual problems and will not uncover the whole tissue which has obviously been pressing upon me for some time in the shape of depressions and inhibitions. On the other hand I am not clear whether it is practicable to begin all over again with a new and this time thoroughly trained analyst–and with whom? And finally, I am longing to get down to my work. Autumn and early winter have always been good productive times for me. So I am in a bit of a quandary with the phenomenon which is certainly like the crystal gazing you quote. By the way, I see while I dictate this letter lying down as I like doing that you are quite right, and that there really is a wish within me to die

[1] *Weltbühne*: Berlin literary periodical.

and to enter into the peace of death and thus escape certain small conflicts which are associated with the realm of one's fathers, i.e., which are of a financial nature. On the one hand I am building myself a small study on the edge of the wood and this must be paid for; on the other hand, the rôle of the paterfamilias has now passed on to me, and my brothers and sisters, some of them heads of families themselves, expect material support from me. On the other hand again, I am obliged to show that I am not mean; and as I can write out a cheque with the greatest ease, since that does not look like money, and I part with a bank note very unwillingly because that is real money—so I prefer to seek refuge in the tomb in order to escape the demands of life and of my family—not to mention those of the state and the income tax people. This piece of analysis has relieved and amused me very much.

You must have derived a grim enjoyment from getting those messages of condolence. It is part and parcel of your very courageous way of life to come to terms with an illness which could be interpreted as professionally damaging. You now have all the more right to be left in peace and to be protected from the literary psychologists. You no doubt realize that it was you who snuffed out the light of Viennese literature, whose raison d'être lay in its psychological insight and its joy in linguistic innovations. You have shown that the human soul has, as it were, seven storeys and that the Viennese writers had done nothing more than describe nicely the colour of the roof. But with incomparably greater perspicacity, accuracy and vividness than anyone else—including Arthur Schnitzler,[1] whom I like and admire warmly as man and writer—you have given expression to what was hitherto hidden from our knowledge. Others will find themselves, I fear, as defenceless when faced with the intellectual content of analysis, its scope, its factual richness and its revelatory power as when confronted with the intellectual

[1] Arthur Schnitzler (1862–1931): Viennese writer and dramatist.

phenomenon of Nietzsche. At that time I was in a particularly embarrassing position, as I had just published a volume of essays called *Lessing, Kleist, Büchner*,[1] which seemed to me very much better than the *Nietzsche, Kleist, Hölderlin*[2] book. When I say this I am in no way oblivious of how difficult it is to establish a livelihood as an intellectual writer of integrity, when one's subconscious remains completely unclassified and sealed up, and how difficult it is to irrigate one's garden with the meagre trickles which manage to escape one's repressions, while the real productive sources remain similarly immured. I carry on an irregular correspondence with Stefan Zweig. I expressed my criticism of his book on Nietzsche quite frankly, but in public I was silent. That will, I fear, not be possible in future.

This is your reward for your kind, I might almost say paternal letter: you get treatises and almost books from me in return. I do not need to tell you that you are the only person I would presume to do this to and to whom I dare speak so openly, without beating about the bush. When you were living here in Tegel, in pain and without anything to do, I meant to send you the little manuscript containing the dreams I had in Oberbozen, one of which at least makes really amusing reading. I really shall do so soon, and I am only waiting till I have added my explanatory notes to this one which I have called the *Pergamon von Suschak*. It did me a lot of good to dream that dream.

And now I hear suddenly that the newspapers have reported the death of your mother. Someone like you who has drawn aside the curtains of life and who has lived as long as you have, speaks his own specific language with death. All the same the death of a mother, even if she has

[1] A. Zweig: *Lessing, Kleist, Büchner: Drei Versuche*. J. M. Späth Verlag, Berlin, 1925.
[2] Stefan Zweig: *Der Kampf mit dem Dämon: Hölderlin, Kleist, Nietzsche*. Insel Verlag, Leipzig, 1925.

reached a great age, is a rupture which causes pain to a son. And this pain I share with you.

With these sentiments I remain

Yours

Arnold Zweig

Vienna IX, Berggasse 19

22. 10. 1930

My dear Mr. Zweig,

I read your little comedy[1] just before I took to my bed for a week (with a temperature). I am far from saying that it had any influence on my illness. But perhaps my illness influenced my judgement of the comedy. For it was not to my taste, above all I did not find it at all funny, and on account of the differences between North and South German I had difficulties in finding my way through the dialogue. I hope you will not take my objections amiss; at least you will know that when I next praise passionately something you have sent me, it will be meant seriously.

I hope that my good wishes for your health and that of your wife will arrive at a more opportune moment than yours did with me.

Ever yours

Freud

[1] A. Zweig: *Laubheu und keine Bleibe*. Gustav Kiepenheuer Verlag, Berlin, 1930.

Professor Sigmund Freud
Internationaler Psychoanalytischer Verlag
Vienna 1
Börsegasse 11

Dear Sir,

I would like to draw your attention to the enclosed documents.[1]

I should be grateful if after giving them your consideration you could see your way to appending your signature to the enclosed manifesto and thus support an important good cause which is to be brought to the notice of the Soviet government and of world opinion.

Yours faithfully
Arnold Zweig

Dear Mr. Freud,

From your letter I gathered first and foremost and with a certain shock that you were ill in bed. But I hope the illness is now over and that the wonderful November we have been granted here has permitted you to drive up to the Kobenzl and enjoy some sunshine, so that the winter will pass without further trouble.

The trouble with *Laubheu und keine Bleibe* is just as you outlined it. The play is neither completely comic nor completely tragic, and its styles really are intermingled. I hoped that this would be overcome on the stage by the skill of the actor, on which we are after all forced to rely to a certain extent. What I like about the play is that it gives visual and symbolic expression to psychical forces such as transference

[1] See Freud's letter of 26. xi. 30.

20

and the break-through of repressed actions, in fact the repetition of an act which has been performed and then repressed, without my having in the least intended it.

With the theatre in its present state this nine-year-old play will probably have to celebrate its bar mitzvah[1] before it is even put on–that is why I sent it to you.

With best wishes and regards to you and your family, in which my wife also joins.

Ever yours
Arnold Zweig

Vienna IX, Berggasse 19
26. xi. 1930

Dear Mr. Zweig,

I have received two documents from you: a sheet headed 'Manifesto' and a memorandum dated 'Berlin. Beginning of January.' I assume that you want my signature just for the first of these. I would give it gladly, did not the manifesto contain an attack on 'the capitalistic economic confusion'. For that would be tantamount to giving my support to the Communist ideal, and I am far from wishing to do that. In spite of all my dissatisfaction with the present economic systems I have no hope that the road pursued by the Soviets will lead to improvement. Indeed any such hope that I may have cherished has disappeared in this decade of Soviet rule. I remain a liberal of the old school. In my last book[2] I criticised uncompromisingly the mixture of despotism and Communism. I do not know whether the Russian dictators pay any attention to the utterances of a few 'intellectuals'– probably they do not give a brass farthing for them–but if they do, then the effect of the manifesto could only

[1] Bar mitzvah: Jewish confirmation ceremony; i.e. the play will be 13 years old before it is performed.

[2] The reference is to *Civilization and its Discontents*. *St. Ed.* XXI, pp. 64 ff.

21

be damaged by the signature of a declared opponent like myself.

Still less of course can I say that I am in agreement with the opinions expressed in the longer pamphlet. I am sorry to have to refuse you anything, and I send you both my warmest greetings.

Yours
Freud

Berlin-Grunewald
Zikadenweg 59
2 December 30

Dear Mr. Freud,

First of all, I perceive with relief from your letter that you are better, since you have written in your own hand and in your usual firm, calm style. I understand only too well your reservations and the reason for your refusal. I myself do not pin much hope on the result of the whole affair, but people from Russia arrived begging us to support their comrades in their struggle by means of our manifesto to which, unlike myself, they attached great significance. It did not seem humanly possible to me not to comply with the appeal of these valiant people.

You can see what I think of Stalinist Russia, if you care to read two essays[1] which I published in the *Weltbühne* on the occasion of the most recent executions. A surge of arguments for and against ensued; the writers who want to seem up to date were enraged because for them everything connected with Russia is taboo. But the capitalistic economic confusion is not made any better because the Communist dictatorship has produced such frightful consequences, nor by the fact that for you in Vienna the ample comfortable standard of living of the middle classes, which the wretched war lowered

[1] A. Zweig: 'Die Moskauer Hinrichtungen'. *Die Weltbühne*, 1930, Heft 46. 'Macht oder Freiheit?' *Die Weltbühne*, 1930, Heft 48.

so much, is now lowered yet further by socialist administration. We are living in difficult years of transition and no one knows where it will lead. The militant character of our society, where class is set against class, grows more and more undisguised. We used to seek refuge in an ideology of flight—flight into the future, i.e. socialism, flight from modern society, whose discontents you have illuminated so brilliantly, flight into a Rousseauistic Zionism. Gradually it is dawning upon us that there can be no flight, that these oppositions must be fought out, and in our own generation, I fear. I am not delighted at the prospect; as an artist I need a peaceful atmosphere without any pressure except that of the problems of form and structure in my books. But as you see, we are not consulted. My thoughts are constantly returning to the theme of an essay I would like to write, if I had time, about your relationship to Nietzsche. To me it seems that you have achieved everything that Nietzsche intuitively felt to be his task, without his being really able to achieve it with his poetic idealism and brilliant inspirations. He tried to explain the birth of tragedy; you have done it in *Totem and Taboo*.[1] He longed for a world beyond Good and Evil; by means of analysis you have discovered a world to which this phrase actually applies. Analysis has reversed all values, it has conquered Christianity, disclosed the true Antichrist, and liberated the spirit of resurgent life from the ascetic ideal.

Analysis has reduced the will to power to what lies at its basis. Indeed in particular questions, which much preoccupied Nietzsche, concerning the linguistic origin of moral concepts, analysis has attacked and resolved infinitely larger and more important problems of speech and expression, of thought association and communication. The purely logical intellect, which Nietzsche called the Socratic and rejected, you have assigned and confined much more precisely to the limited area of the conscious mind. And thanks to the fact that you are a scientist, and furthermore a psychologist who

[1] S. Freud: *Totem and Taboo. St. Ed.* XIII.

advances step by step, you have attained what Nietzsche would so gladly have achieved himself: the scientific description and explanation of the human soul – and more than that, since you are a physician, you have taught and created the possibility of influencing and curing it. I believe too that a large number of particular observations, which concern for instance the writer Freud, provide links with Nietzsche, and that the intrepidity of Nietzsche 'who philosophises with the hammer' has been far out-stripped by the courage which sought out and revealed the Orphic and Dionysiac concepts of Nietzsche in the simple and objective respects in which they are still alive in each of us today.

Unfortunately I am unable, at any rate, just at present, to write this essay, because I find it impossible at present – and for the next few years – to master all the material. But this is a pity, for the world would certainly be ready to listen, for it has a passion for putting things in order and does not understand things till it can classify them. Now it would be splendid if you were to make a study of the real 'will to power', that is to say the politicians' lust for power in the sociological struggle, and if you were to pursue it in one of your little yellow books[1] from its conscious ideological stage right down to the depths. Then the cycle of the Freud-Nietzsche relationship would be complete. If you know of anyone in the position to treat the subject which I have sketched well, i.e. thoroughly, and with an easy command of the material, I would gladly put these first outlines at his disposal. We are now entering the darkest time of the year, in every sense of the word, I fear, and I do not know whether I should envy you, because you must feel the hardships of the present situation more acutely than do the likes of us.

With warmest greetings and good wishes

Yours
Arnold Zweig

[1] Some of the volumes of the Internationaler Psychoanalytischer Verlag appeared in yellow bindings.

Dear Mr. Zweig,

I was very pleased to find the old warm note in your letter, though I have recently sent you nothing but refusals.

What you say about the Soviet experiment strikes an answering chord in me. We have been deprived by it of a hope—and an illusion—and we have received nothing in exchange. We are moving towards dark times: the apathy of old age ought to enable me to rise above it all, but I cannot help the fact that I am sorry for my seven grandchildren.

I cannot write the yellow book you wish me to. I know too little about the human drive for power, for I have lived my life as a theorist. I am constantly surprised at the tendencies of recent years, which have carried me so far into the world of topical current affairs. Indeed I would like to write nothing more, and yet I am once again writing an Introduction[1] for something someone else is doing. I must not say what it is, but it too is an analysis and at the same time very much a matter of contemporary interest, almost political. You will never guess what.

I shall get your essays here. The one on the links between Nietzsche's influence and mine you should certainly write; I don't need to read it. You could write it when I am no longer here and you are haunted by the memory of me. That you should hand over your material on this subject to someone else is out of the question; and who should it be anyway? I know of no one.

I am not satisfied with my prosthesis, but I have no intention of going to Berlin on that account. I don't suppose I would get anything better there. So I shall not be seeing

[1] Introduction to a study of Woodrow Wilson, by W. C. Bullitt: *Thomas Woodrow Wilson, twenty-eighth President of the United States*; first published 1967.

25

you nor your wife, nor my children and their families for some time. But do write again.

With warmest greetings

Yours

Freud

Eichkamp

27. xii. 1930

Dear Mr. Freud,

You did not want to put me to the test, I'm sure—why should you? You know that it is your life's work which first made mine possible and that I am happy to be able to feel this and to express it to you now and then. Today I take up my fountain pen to do it—and the pen does not seem to approve of this wretched paper at all—and I come out with a New Year greeting which naturally must begin with the word 'may'. So may the year 1931 bring you, along with its inevitable troubles, as much joy as the one which has just passed. You have the right to pity your grandchildren; we, a generation who are hardened in every sense of the word, are determined to get on with this wretched life, taking it just as it is, and not to look for unpleasantnesses and also not to stick it out just out of heroism, but to seek out what is pleasant as man always has done. I have now changed my pen; now things are going smoothly; if mistakes occur, if I write m for n or vice versa—that is because my eye is unable to control the speed of my pen.

Your introduction makes me curious about what it introduces. Today I come to you with a request, which you will certainly not misunderstand. In the next few weeks I shall be moving into a workroom, which I have had built near our all too small house. There, for the first time in my life there will be room for all my books and even space for new purchases of editions in many volumes. If I order a set of your *Gesammelte Schriften* from your Verlag through Kiepenheuer, in order to avoid the bookseller's commission, would you write your name for me in either Vol. I or the last volume? Just as a token from your hand in your own work. Such a personal touch goes far beyond the lifetime of the individual and lives on, ever productive.

We shall think of you over a glass of wine on New Year's Eve and shall send you our best wishes.

As always
Yours
Arnold Zweig

Vienna IX, Berggasse 19
30. xii. 1930

Dear Mr. Zweig,

Of course! I am writing to the Verlag today to tell them that when the order comes through from Kiepenheuer, they are to send me Vol. I for me to make my mark on the title page.

This card takes advantage of the date and of an age-old superstition of omnipotence to wish you and yours a happy 1931.

As ever
Yours
Freud

Vienna IX, Berggasse 19
10. 5. 1931

Dear Mr. Zweig,

I wished—and indeed I still wish—to reproach you for having so carelessly let yourself in for superfluous ailments of your various organs and functions, as your letter darkly hints,[1] but it has occurred to me in time that I am not the right person to criticize you on this score. For on April 24th

---

[1] Reference to an unpublished letter.

I had to undergo a further operation for a growth fundamentally similar to the one I had eight years ago, and this
has robbed me of a good deal of my energy, and today after
what I have gone through I am weak, hors de combat,
impeded in my speech, a mere shadow of my former self.
Well-meaning friends advise me to choose another exit
from life rather than this particular form of relapse. I am
in agreement with them, but quite without influence on
further developments.

Tomorrow I shall make my first attempt to creep back to
work. An hour in the morning and another in the afternoon.
Living one's life for one's health and guarded like a historical
monument is otherwise hard to bear.

As soon as my treatments allow me the time I shall yield
to the temptation of reading your 18 stories.[1] Good things
are in store for me, I'm sure. You should pursue your
phantasies with patience. You will discover an astonishing
amount and probably gain a great respect for the poetic
capabilities of your unconscious. But do not expect to get
through it too quickly. Such wealth is not easily exhausted.
I advise you to keep clear of all further dilettantish experiments with illness and I send warm greetings to you and
your wife.

Yours
Freud

Vienna IX, Berggasse 19
10. 12. 31

Dear Mr. Zweig,

Thank you for your fine book.[2] My time is taken up with
my treatments, both active and passive, and so I am taking
small sips of it in my free half-hours. Every little chapter is a

---

[1] A. Zweig: *Knaben und Männer* (18 stories). Gustav Kiepenheuer
Verlag, Berlin, 1931.

[2] English translation: *Young Woman of 1914*. Martin Secker, 1932.

delicious morsel. It is true that so far I am still in the idyllic prologue; I imagine it will get more tragic. When I have finished it, I will write to you with my usual candour. Somehow I conclude from the words of your dedication (glad to have got as far as that) that your eyes and therefore you yourself are in good fettle and I trust I am not wrong in this.

There is little to report about myself, little that would be worth telling; my vitality is diminishing to a peculiar degree, etc. etc.

Kiepenheuer's offer is very tempting for its advertisement value, but it would be suicidal for the Internationaler Verlag to take it up. Naturally he wants the book that is doing best, the *Introductory Lectures*. I am in the very act of pulling the Verlag out of the abyss of bankruptcy by means of donations and considerable financial sacrifices of my own, and I cannot impose such a renunciation (for only 7500 marks) upon it. I would not risk a single mark in the Nobel Prize stakes.

Well, I wish you a good, happy and stimulating journey and please send a little card now and then to

your sincerely devoted
Freud

Berlin-Grunewald
Zikadenweg 59
11. 12. 31

Dear Mr. and Father Freud,

By this time my book will have reached you and will have accounted for the worst part of my long silence. It is only a fragment of a fragment, though, it's true, it has been rounded off and given shape. I think I am lucky because I possess just sufficient Mediterranean Jewish ingredients in my make-up to enable me to introduce order and form into the organic activity of my imagination. I have not got as much of this as your compatriots who from sheer formalism never succeed in evolving true form—or rather I should alas say evolved, in the past tense. For the late Hofmannsthal[1] to whom this 'alas' refers seems to me deeply to be pitied. I do not regret other dead writers who also left this world with their work unfinished nearly as much as I do this highly gifted man, of whom at most a few poems and the memory of his intellectual calibre will remain. But this is just a parenthesis, evoked perhaps by Arthur Schnitzler's death about which I have not as yet been able to say a word—to anyone. For he bore a physical resemblance to my father, except that my father was a country type of Jew. His *Weg ins Freie*[2] once meant more to me than all the rest of his works or those of his contemporaries.

Now I move on to something more pleasant, which is nevertheless shrouded in feelings of guilt for me: your seventy-fifth birthday. I sent the *Weltbühne* an essay arising from two small matters of current interest and also connected with your theoretical writings, which were being read aloud to me then, until my proof correcting deprived me of leisure for anything else. This journal, to which I have been faithful since 1912, has still not published my essay, and now the two points of current import both need a commentary and I do not know whether I shall be able to publish it as it now stands. The manners of this generation are queer and fame has durability only in the dried up form of the newspaper cuttings which my secretary lays before me just to pack them away again.

Meanwhile I have had occasion and opportunity to allow my two little sons to benefit from the blessings of your creative discoveries. One of them revealed a great deal of himself in his drawings and paintings. By means of these I was able to establish contact with him and conversations at table about food helped to provide an outlet for the repressed

[1] Hugo v. Hofmannsthal (1874–1929): Austrian poet.
[2] Published 1908.

material. The result was simply overwhelming. At school he was suddenly awarded one Grade II after another and his paintings changed from the daemonic into the enchanting. After each of our conversations he dashed off in a burst of song–perhaps one day I shall be able to show you his paintings, either when you next come to Tegel or when we visit Austria. With my other son things move slowly. I would like him to have treatment from someone else, but unfortunately I have not heard from Frau B. though I have written her two letters, or to be more precise, one card and one letter. The burden these cursed Nazis lay upon a child's mind is sad. I am now preparing a new edition of *Caliban*, turning it from academic language into German, so that politicians can read it. Unfortunately I am confirmed in all that I saw in 1920.

And now, farewell. Every day really I am busy with matters that pertain to you and my association with you means that my thoughts are constantly turning towards you. My eyes are now, alas, supposed to take a rest, so I have not yet cut the pages of Frau Lou's[1] book.[2] But in such beautiful sunshine I cannot deprive myself of the luxury of writing to you, and writing to you is not really a luxury, but the one great pleasure of a man who was once upon a time a passionate letter-writer.

And so with greetings to your wife and daughter in which my wife also joins, I am with all my heart

Ever yours
Arnold Zweig

P.S. This old notepaper comes from some Russian documents; it may well be older than you, dating back to 1850.

P.P.S. I wrote this letter this morning. At midday your letter arrived. I am so pleased that our feelings crossed in this way.

[1] Lou Andreas-Salomé (1861–1937): Writer and psychoanalyst.
[2] *Mein Dank an Freud*. Internationaler Psychoanalytischer Verlag, Vienna, 1931.

I think four years of war were worse than anything we have now. The children too were more to be pitied than they are today. You can have lice, live in a hole in the ground, eat mouldy bread, as we did for a long time—the very feeling of being alive makes it worth while having been born.

Yours

Zw.

Vienna IX, Berggasse 19

7. 1. 32

Dear A. Z.,

My wife thinks that the photograph of an old Jew sent you at Christmas cannot have reached you. I am just writing to ask whether I should send a replacement.

Ever yours

Freud

Berlin-Grunewald

8. 1. 32

Dear and revered Mr. Freud,

You know yourself how much pleasure you gave to me and to my wife with this photo of an old Jew. Your well-known features—a little more ascetic but with undiminished energy in both expression and bearing, without any of the false "resignation" of the years. Nothing has given me so much pleasure since the appearance of *Junge Frau*. If I did not write straightaway and thank you and turn to you—inwardly I was doing it all the time—it was just because I was waiting to see whether I would not be able to tell you that I would soon be coming to thank you personally. For I am supposed to be delivering another lecture in Vienna and that might easily be combined with a holiday in the mountains. But in connection with all this a lot has to be fitted in and so as yet I have not accepted the invitation.

You have no idea how close I feel to you just now. I have taken up my analysis again in order to finish it – but not with Dr. K., who is too passive and who is not yet quite at home in your world, but with Dr. S. with whom I have much in common through our Upper Silesian origins. Things are going marvellously well as far as resistance and resolution are concerned and behind all the individual hours your figure and face emerge like a vast veiled statue – the face of that old Jew who has not feared to penetrate the repressions of a whole human epoch. You see, I am almost falling into the 'Freud and Nietzsche' essay which I have started and laid aside once again in order to finish my analysis first. But then . . .!

Yours
Arnold Zweig

Greetings to your wife and to Anna Freud, to whom I have something nice to show when I come.

Berlin-Grunewald
Zikadenweg 59
28. 1. 32

Dear Mr. Freud,

Unfortunately the Zionist ladies who wanted to have me speak in Vienna have already got their full complement of speakers for February and as Jakob Wassermann[1] also wants to speak on a topic on which actually I think I would have more to say, i.e. the needs of youth today, I have no alternative but to postpone my visit to you. This I do with a heavy heart, as I wanted very much to see you again to tell you of the experiences I have had or shall soon have had with the very efficient and talented Dr. S. My good Dr. K. was of too passive a nature and too unaccustomed to using the amazing intellectual apparatus you have evolved to be able, to quote

[1] Jakob Wassermann (1873–1941): German novelist.

Nietzsche, 'to help those perhaps most in need of help', those who are sick in feeling and mind and who are unable to resolve on their own the contradiction between nature and civilisation. Well, that certainly exceeds the ability of any individual, and consequently the effect of analysis will only be seen when it can work on the broad basis which it will conquer as its right and due.

That reminds me that my publisher, young Dr. Fritz Landshoff, told me that the firm of Kiepenheuer is negotiating with you about a cheap popular edition of some of your basic works. I must say nothing would seem to me more appropriate for opening the attack on the broad front which will one day inevitably establish analysis in the general consciousness of mankind. It is true that the payment on each individual copy is ridiculously low, and if we could succeed in reducing the claims made by the booksellers, who expect to earn seven or perhaps eight times more per copy than we get, then the rôle of the writer and consequently of the intellectual in society would be improved. But if you are interested in wide publicity for a section of your works, this method of a Kiepenheuer popular edition would not seem to me to be a bad choice. It is true that he does very little advertising, which causes the reactionary press to reproach us, his authors, with the fact that we owe our reputation abroad only to propaganda–but at any rate this would be a step outside the specialist circle and it would bring analysis to the notice of people who learn about it now only at sixth or seventh hand. You know, too, that I consider it a scandal that you have not yet been awarded the Nobel Prize. But the Scandinavians are, as I put it in conversation yesterday, intellectually of an amazing naïveté, and they do what they can to avoid specialist publications. Were they to be confronted with a special popular edition of your works as well as your impressive collected opus then perhaps the Christians of this Protestant nation might be enlisted on your behalf.

So I am postponing my visit to you, but I hope definitely to see you either in spring or summer wherever you may be and where I hope I shall find you well and prepared to receive me, an outsider, but one who judged by his feelings is certainly an insider. Instead of coming to Vienna I am now going with my wife to Marseilles and thence to Palestine —a visit which is long overdue and which I am trying to make as unofficial as possible. After that I intend to make a public expression of my views on the Jewish question and bring out a new edition of *Caliban*, which is the only work I am taking with me on this journey.

I will bring with me when I come the little present for you and your daughter, to which I referred in my last letter. It consists of the drawings and paintings of my little son Adam who as a seven-year-old boy suffered from a phobia about robbers, burglars, dark rooms and death and whom I tried very carefully and cautiously to help. The surprising thing is that these pictures changed completely in character before and after the analysis and in such a way that his talent was not destroyed by the analysis but fully liberated for the first time. A proof which astonished everyone to whom I showed this material. But more of this later. Today just the warmest greetings for you and your family. I hope you will come through the winter all right and that you will give us the opportunity of spending some time in your company in this, the Goethe year.

Yours
Zweig

Vienna IX, Berggasse 19
29. 1. 32

Dear Mr. Zweig,

An answer by return on account of your imminent departure. No line from the whole Renaissance is clearer in my memory than Lorenzo the Magnificent's: Di doman' non c'e certan,[1] and so I cannot fully rejoice that you are going to Palestine instead of Vienna, though I too would like to make such an exchange. We are thinking of spending the summer once again in the beautiful Mauthner house in Pötzleinsdorf (Vienna XVIII), and we look forward to being able to entertain you both in our garden there as we did in Tegel.

The times are not propitious for any production from me; your production must not be interrupted.

Warmest greetings from all of us to you, your wife who is returning home and to Frl. O.

Yours
Freud

Haifa
16. 2. 32

Dear Mr. Freud,

From the house of my friend Struck[2] at the height of the spring we send you our kindest greetings and good wishes. We hear your city now and then on the wireless at night and we think of you affectionately and with some concern, when we hear the weather reports. But you will get through this winter weather and have just as lovely a spring as we are having here. This is the wish of my wife and myself and we send our greetings too to all your family.

Yours
Arnold Zweig

Eichkamp
1 May 32

Dear and honoured man,

We have been home now for three weeks and this is the first quiet hour I have had alone. No children, no wife,

---

[1] 'Nothing is certain about tomorrow.'
[2] Hermann Struck (1876–1944): Painter and engraver.

neither my sister nor my secretary, just the familiar brown cigar and the pale blue light of a cold spring day outside my window—and at once, instead of reading something as I meant to or working away at my new book, I find my way to you to announce my return. It is strange how I think about you in your big flat among your books and the treasures that have risen from the tombs, whose place of origin I have just been visiting. I could not settle down—apart from the children of course—a new creative idea had developed in me following on the war novels (or rather it is an old idea, dating back to 22 or 24, but suddenly it was there all complete) so that I could not pick up the threads of my work. And between me and some of the people I was looking forward to seeing again lay all the bustle of the wide world in which they had had no part and the tumult of the unbridled, distorted folly, which we had been away from. As I walked round my study the feeling came over me: what a mistake to try to come back here! What remains intact at this moment of the Europe I love and of the Germany to which I in large part belong, the original source of my strength and of my work? Why did I not stay over there in the heroic scenery of Galilee or by the sea at Tel Aviv or at the Dead Sea or in the idyllic landscape of Méadie near Cairo, where there are such wonderful bougainvillaea trees, purple canopies of blossom, as big as a good-sized acacia? Then on my desk I saw your photo, which my secretary has meantime fixed between two sheets of glass on a metal base, and this was such a greeting from the heart of the creative zone, from warmth and goodness of heart and from the great European tradition of Reason, that I turned on my heel with a sigh and a smile and said to myself: Now you must first deal with all the post that has come, then start on your new work and just stay here and not run away. Freud too has not run away. And that is what I have done.

Naturally I have not as yet committed myself absolutely

to any *one* piece of work, both novels are running round in my head, but they are nearly separated from one another and they are only squabbling for precedence. One of them[1] takes place in Palestine and portrays the tragic figure of the great, strange Orthodox poet, Jacob Israel de Haan, who lived in Jerusalem to revile God there, and who was murdered by a Chalutz[2] because his hatred of political Jewry had turned him into a traitor and informer.

The other novel[3] is to portray the world at the outbreak of the war, as it is seen through the eyes of a young war volunteer; he feels things like a character from Stendhal and sees it all quite objectively. But it is also told from the point of view of an officer of the Prussian General Staff who experiences the loss of the Battle of the Marne and afterwards witnesses the senseless mowing down of the whole of German youth. He cannot prevent this and takes the frightful burden of silence upon himself and collapses under it. As you see, I am not dealing with trifles, but the choice between these two is a difficult one for me to make, and at the back of my mind two other novels are waiting and my heart clings to both of them and would cling even if there had been no 1914: the Solomon novel, which is to describe the world of prehistoric times, and *Die Hemmung*, which is to depict modern man in his totality, the novel of analysis.

My eyes are much better; my horizon has widened; I could, it is true, be more relaxed, but I feel I am in possession of all my faculties—and if the weather is kind, I should have a good summer and produce something worth while. And with that I shall say goodbye to you for today and I hope to have a few lines from you soon; meantime I am going to get

---

[1] English translation: *De Vriendt Goes Home.*

[2] Chalutz: Jewish immigrant to Palestine who worked as pioneer in settlements.

[3] English translation: *Education before Verdun.* Viking, 1936; Secker & Warburg, 1936.

a photograph taken which I will send you with the pictures of my studio.

All good wishes to you and your family.

Yours
Arnold Zweig

Eichkamp
4 May 32

Dear Mr. Freud,

I have just seen that I was right in having a vague feeling that your birthday was approaching, though it is true I thought it was at the end of the month. But now I see it is on the sixth (the same day as my brother's) and I am happy to think that I wrote of my own accord without knowing this. When anyone has got as far as you have, there are not many wishes left to wish him and one can give him only a symbolic gift. But I can at least wish you a good and sunny spring and a year free from pain. And this I do, also at the behest of my wife who does not like writing letters, and I add my greetings to all your family.

Yours
Arnold Zweig

Hochroterd
8. v. 32

Dear Meister Arnold,

Where am I writing from? From a small farmhouse on a hillside, forty-five minutes by car from the Berggasse, which my daughter and her American friend[1] (who owns the car) have bought and furnished as a weekend cottage. We had expected that your journey home from Palestine would take you through Vienna and then we would have insisted on your seeing it.

[1] Mrs. Dorothy Burlingham: Psychoanalyst.

You have been very generous in sending me your picture, though it is true it does not show me much of you except your forehead, and also the photograph of your author's cage[1] which I shall never manage to see, together with the news that your eyes have improved and those few drops from the cauldron where so many new stories are now brewing—all of which I would like to read though my days are beginning to be numbered.

You were right; I have just had my birthday and now I am laboriously defending myself against the obligations arising from it. But to come back to you—how strange this tragically mad land you have visited must have seemed to you. Just think, this strip of our mother earth is connected with no other progress, no discovery or invention—the Phoenicians are said to have invented glass and the alphabet (both doubtful!), the island of Crete gave us Minoan art, Pergamon reminds us of parchment, Magnesia of the magnet and so on ad infinitum—but Palestine has never produced anything but religions, sacred frenzies, presumptuous attempts to overcome the outer world of appearance by means of the inner world of wishful thinking. And we hail from there (though one of us considers himself a German as well; the other does not); our forebears lived there for perhaps half or perhaps a whole millennium (but this too is just a perhaps) and it is impossible to say what heritage from this land we have taken over into our blood and nerves (as is mistakenly said). Oh, life could be very interesting if we only knew and understood more about it. But we are sure only of our feelings of the moment—among mine are my sincere good wishes for you and your work.

With greetings to your wife

Yours
Freud

[1] Referring to the modern studio which had been built for Arnold Zweig by the Berlin architect Harry Rosenthal.

Dear and honoured man,

You have replied to my letter so quickly, at such length and with so much perceptiveness that I have been pre-occupied ever since with my reply to you, though I have not, it is true, been able to take any active steps in the matter. On the contrary, I have had to deal with a whole mass of trifling affairs, unrewarding and yet time-consuming: a radio talk to America, which was, it is true, technically amusing, on the theme 'Has Europe fought its last battle?' It was a tedious business writing it in English and fitting it into the time (17-18 minutes); a radio talk in Berlin for the P.E.N. Club, an address to the P.E.N. Club, and then immediately after this I had to make all the arrangements for a disappear-ance of 3-4 weeks. And in the midst of it all the decision about my work for this summer–it is to be not a long novel but a shorter and quite different one, so that what I wrote you about must wait till later. And now I have been here about nine days, of which only one and a half have been fine. I am deep in my work and equally deep in depression, which is connected with the rain, with Bavarian memories, with the grey sky, the terrible political situation in Berlin, with my physical exhaustion after my long journey, but above all with the theme of my work itself. This is the shorter novel dealing with the murder of the Dutch-Jewish writer, J. I. de Haan, in Jerusalem (1924) and the Arab revolt of 1929. The theme has been in my mind for a long time. The figure of this Orthodox Jew who 'reviled God in Jerusalem' in clandestine poems and who had a love-affair with an Arab boy–this important and complex character gripped my imagination while the blood was still not dry in the whole affair. My trip to Palestine brought the old plan to life again and for a month I sketched away at it in the country itself and made a quite useful and indeed fascinating plan for it. Only to discover some ten days later there was a flaw at the most vital spot—de Haan was not murdered by Arabs at all, as I had believed for seven years, but by a Jew, a political opponent, a radical Zionist, known to many people and still living in the country today. I realise now what a frightful blow to me this was—at first I did not take it in. I laid a new foundation for my work; this new fact was far better than the old; it compelled me to see things accurately without pro-Jewish prejudice and to examine the political murder of one Jew by another exactly as though it were a political murder in Germany; it compelled me to tread the path of disillusionment yet further, as far as necessary, or possible—further than was good for me.

You see I *am* answering your letter, but first I want to spin out my thread yet further. The homosexual component in this book, which I am dictating with special distaste and with specially great concentration, challenged me right away to self-analysis. I was both, the Arab (semitic) boy and the impious-Orthodox lover and writer. I am afraid that the removal of these repressions is the main cause for my depression. That is going a little far, isn't it? Must one always pay with the few pleasures life offers once one touches one's own taboos, even though one has seen it all quite clearly analytically? Knowledge is of no avail. The liberated instinct wants to live its life right through emotionally, in phantasy, in the flesh and blood of the mind and an author, ridiculous fellow that he is, really does not need his 'author's cage' as you so strikingly put it—he has always got it inside him.

We are now hidden in the clouds once again.

You are no doubt back in Vienna once more; I do not know whether I shall stick it out here this week. As far as my work is concerned I would very much like to. The book is meant to appear in the autumn but I would like to send it to you before that, in typescript if I do not make too many alterations. I already feel much better now that I have written all this to you—you read so between the lines and indeed inside the sheet of paper itself.

You touched on two difficult points which I have thought about a great deal. My relationship to Germany and to my Germanness, and my relationship to the Jews, to the Jewishness in me and in the world, and to Palestine. This land of religions can, after all, be seen from other points of view than just as a land of delusions and desires, and especially by you. I have always found that in the human economy, religion marks the attempt to canalise man's vast instinctual reservoir into rational activity—maybe it is a premature attempt and yet that is not true since one cannot begin this attempt too soon. It seemed and still seems to me that the meaningful coordination of the instincts is the creative factor in religion, the great transformation of man with a view to a constructive life, and the intellectual systems which have formulated the meaning and purpose of life here seemed to me less important (because they are transitory) than the splendid urge which prompts us to settle our problems with our fellow men in a moral way. Is this impulse not inborn within us? Have not we, the Jews, produced this impulse in many more individuals than has any other modern race? Is not the frightful struggle you have been waging for about forty years (or more?) against the fallacies, taboos and repressions of our contemporaries comparable with the one the prophets waged against the recalcitrant nation of their day? Your radiantly clear intelligence shifts the nature of man and the purpose of his development on to an incomparably more realistic plane than did the people of those days, who could only murmur the word 'God'—but apart from this, I see much in common between you. And we certainly have our Germanness in common—only it's a Germanness of the past, it seems to me. I am just as much a German as a Jew in my excavations into the war years: as a German who cannot bear to see this nation carrying round with it a false, trashy, vain image of its great and frightful achievements and suffering, and as a Jew who defends himself against the reproaches made by the anti-semitic German about the Jews and their part in the war. And the higher union of both these—our poor imperilled Europe and ultimately the round globe itself on which we as good citizens are voyaging into the Infinite.

I hope your voyage is going well these days; all my heart is in this wish! For you see the fact of Man as it is, I am only just learning to do so and so I have to put up with a good deal of annoyance.

But my best wishes to you! I hope the sun is shining in Vienna. That is the sincere wish of your

Arnold Zweig

Vienna IX, Berggasse 19
18. 8. 1932

Dear Meister Arnold

(I think you shall keep this name)

I was very uncertain as to where I should write to you, for I cannot make up my mind about your Berlin addresses—Eichkamp or Grunewald—but you did after all ultimately get the card that went astray at the address which I am using today. I wanted to tell you first that I am pleased that the rumour was exaggerated (but perhaps it was only premature). I mean I had heard that immediately after Einstein's departure for Leiden you too were forced to leave Berlin because of threatening letters. So it is not yet as bad as that. The urge to complete things, which expresses itself in the building of skyscrapers, also loves to turn every hint into the ultimate event. And then I wanted to say to you: send as much as you like and come yourself whenever you want to. I am now working at the new lectures, it's true, but I can do that only for a few hours each day and during the next few weeks I shall have 1–2 analyses at most. Until September 15th we are staying here, where it is very beautiful (XVIII

Khevenhüllerstr. 6) and where you could do your corrections and your imaginings in the garden while your wife exchanged womanly interests with my womenfolk in another part of the park. Then, it is true—or a bit later—there comes our town flat with its limited space. So perhaps the Nazis are playing into my hands for once. When you tell me about your thoughts, I can relieve you of the illusion that one has to be a German. Should we not leave this God-forsaken nation to themselves?

I am going to conclude now so that this letter may reach you more quickly and I send you both my sincere greetings.

Yours
Freud

Eichkamp
16 Nov. 32

Dear Father Freud,

The mountain has been scaled—that is to say, the book is there. On Tuesday it should come out—and since Tuesday is counted as the Jews' lucky day because in the story of the Creation the report inadvertently occurs twice 'and He saw that it was good', I am going to interpret that as a good omen. The book will give offence to Jews and non-Jews alike, since it condemns nationalism and political murder even among Jews, and as I am ridiculously sensitive to public criticism, though I attach no importance to it, I have already got an uneasy feeling—arising from a state of exhaustion after my work.

29 Nov. This letter was interrupted by the news that the book was not to appear on Tuesday and that it contained a number of misprints which had still to be corrected—and with this announcement began a period of irritation for me, too petty to bother you with but unpleasant enough. . . . But now it really is out; you have it in your hands and you will feel how much it owes to you.

I am now in a strange state of mind. Often my disgust at the contradictions in modern man is more than I can stand. Technically he is richly endowed like some kind of insect, but ethically he is undeveloped like a hamster or a mole. He is suffocated by a superabundance of every kind but he is unable to use his social feelings to clear a way for himself out of all the idiotic entanglements of modern life, so that the world we live in makes us the victims of a universal rigidity and of our own impotence and it casts us in the rôle of Cassandra against our own will, because we know it to be of no avail. Fundamentally we are suffering today from the fact that man's religious impulses have been diverted into the metaphysical sphere in order to serve fetishist anxieties and to sustain ecclesiastical hierarchies. I believe that man's religious impulses were destined to the training and disciplining of mass emotions and that they were meant to act as a civilising force in community life. Fear of death and of spirits has made religions what they are, the 'salvation of the soul' has swallowed up the salvation of the living human being and has handed over the state to the armed forces, so that the custodians of the states and their inhabitants are today, as in the time of Saul, on the one hand priests and on the other hand soldiers, and our age which is technically so terrifyingly armed compels our thoroughly uncivilised fellow men to dwell in greater fear than our primitive forebears did, but with the same basic emotions. Perhaps you will sense that unconsciously I am already at work on the task which lies ahead of me, i.e. publishing a new edition of *Caliban*, that is to say, writing it all over again, making it generally intelligible, even for politicians and modern youth and if possible suitable for translation into English.

My own troubles have, in the main, evaporated once more—partly resolved, partly restored to the depressive curves of my normal condition. If one cannot realise one's aggression in the proper place, i.e. in political life against the forces of reaction, it will find its outlet wherever it can and disturb one's private life in its course; and if this outlet through phantasy finds its expression in one's writings, this aggression will be dissolved and will carry off with it at the same time forces which should express themselves in real life, there creating order, establishing connections, overcoming inhibitions, making decisions and surmounting resistances. That is how I now see it and I am putting everything else aside.

For I have recently begun treatment for my right eye and that keeps me in Berlin. A Dr. E., who makes a good impression and is very well thought of by the University of Leningrad, is trying to stimulate the vessels of the membrane to re-absorb the fluid which they used to secrete so prolifically—this he is doing by means of optical diathermy and by the electrolised distribution of medicinal drugs in the eye. As he believes he will achieve some success in the next few weeks and as every new idea fascinates me, I am trying it out. My left eye took seven years before it deigned to function again.

May you flourish as far as it is possible to do so in these times and give a kindly thought now and then to your foster son.

A few little photos by way of greeting!

Arnold Zweig

Vienna IX, Berggasse 19
27. xi. 32

Dear Meister Arnold,

It was not long before I had read your new book right through and the impression it made upon me is still so powerful that I am scarcely in a position yet to say much to you about it. An impression it certainly does make and by the time one has finished it one is satiated with experiences—the material, its wealth, the sharpness of delineation, the absence of bias in the description—all this takes possession of the reader. It is something so entirely different from your usual style. Then one realises that woman scarcely plays any part in the book; that it is a book about a quarrel and a struggle among men and that, quite justifiably, the only love that occurs is the love of a man for a boy. The background—this time a historical one—is, as always with you, masterly. The character into whom you have put your own ego is once again the anchor for the reader; after a few lines he becomes our bosom friend, our interpreter and our guide. Though I doubt whether there are many Englishmen in the Secret Service who are so like Arnold Zweig.

Strangely enough my attention is attracted most potently this time by what in a dream I would call 'day residues'. Surely you have not invented in every detail your de Vriendt and other figures and events. Of course the quatrains are your own invention. Is it a special piece of artistry that many of them read like translations from the Dutch?

As it happens I am able to send you something from us today. I had a hand in editing the book[1] which is going off to you at the same time as this. They are the letters of an uncle[2] of my wife's who was a famous classical scholar and, it appears, an outstanding personality. His attitude towards the Jewish and Christian faiths is worthy of attention. Also his affectionate relationship with Paul Heyse[3]. I beg you to read this little book. In a few days you will receive a copy of my last work, perhaps really the last, a supplement to the *Introductory Lectures*.[4] I have been very low with otitis after an attack of influenza.

And now I send my warmest greetings to you in your busy solitude.

Yours

Freud

[1] Jacob Bernays: *Ein Lebensbild in Briefen*. Edited by Michael Fraenkel. Breslau, Marcus, 1932.
[2] Jacob Bernays (1824–1881): Professor of Classical Philology in Breslau and Bonn.   [3] Paul Heyse (1830–1914): German writer.
[4] Freud: *New Introductory Lectures on Psycho-Analysis. St. Ed.* XXII.

Dear Father Freud,

This time, for the sake of speed, I am typing my letter to you, which seems to me a heartless way for us to correspond but on this occasion I cannot avoid it. Your attack of influenza makes me more concerned than I can say. Would it not be possible, if the weather is as nice with you as it is here—rather cold, very clear, very dry, many hours of sunshine—for you to go and convalesce for a fortnight at one of the beautiful mountain resorts which you have so near you and which I do not know at all? No inflammation of the ear should be allowed to undermine your hearing and the world's access to you—above all you should not speak of your last work any differently from the way the rest of us do when we mean our latest. I hope I shall soon hear from you that you are once again feeling as strong as the handwriting in your latest letter proclaims you to be.

The content of that letter delights me—that you know. I can bear criticism, I exercise some upon myself, but the very proximity of a book just completed makes it impossible to judge its proportions aright (I am almost without judgement when faced with my typescript, I just feel a pleasure in my own creation and the inevitability of its form, but I never dare estimate how far that which I have aimed at has really taken shape) and so your sympathetic understanding seems to me like the first indication that I have succeeded in carrying along with me the most exacting of my readers and my incorruptible friend. The 'day residue' is quickly told, especially if you refer to the essay I published a few days ago in the *Jüdische Rundschau*. My de Vriendt has many features in common with the Dutch poet and journalist, Jacob Israel de Haan, who was murdered by an unknown hand in Jerusalem in 1924. His last work was called *Kwatrijnen* and I have known five of these quatrains in a journalistic prose

49

translation ever since the day when his fate first roused my interest. Orthodox Jew, blasphemer, lover of Arab boys, brilliant writer, lawyer and politician of the Agudath Jisrael,[1] he was in close contact with the Arab princes; he represented the old policy of tolerance, and stabbed the Zionists in the back at every opportunity. He was murdered after he had tried to repress the Zionists in favour of the Agudath before Lord Northcliffe and the Arabs had made a similar attempt. The murderer was never discovered; the Zionist press, to which I belonged at the time, obstinately maintained the view that he had been murdered by the Arabs in connection with his love-affairs. This provided me with the material for a short story which I wanted to write and then forgot. This spring in Palestine it became extraordinarily vivid to me again, and on March 5th I made a sketch for my story on a terrace in Jerusalem. By March 6th this plan had already collapsed: my first enquiry about de Haan's murderer brought the answer that it was not an Arab at all but a Jew who had murdered him and that his identity was known. By March 7th, however, it had become clear that precisely through this collapse my plan had found its true dimension. From then on I began to write; in one month I dictated it on to the stenograph, let it lie for another month after a typescript had been made and then, thanks to the unselfish cooperation of the girl to whom I have dedicated the book ('should I really write that?' she has just asked), it received the form it now has and shall retain.

No more today. It is good that our letters crossed and that we were thinking of one another at the same time and I shall certainly read Jacob Bernays' book. I know too who Jacob Bernays was and I also know Hermann Uhde Bernays[2] of Starnberg. The fact that it is dedicated to you

[1] Society of Orthodox Jews.
[2] Hermann Uhde-Bernays: Stepson of Michael Bernays; painter and art critic.

and is connected with your family makes me specially interested in it.

And now, dear Father Freud, get well again. That is the chief concern of your faithful foster-son

Arnold Zweig

Eichkamp
11. 12. 32

Dear Father Freud,

I have listened with emotion to the introductory words of the third part of the *Lectures*. It seemed as though you were speaking to me through the lips of my secretary and through me to the whole of the contemporary world. To think that you should have to invent a public for yourself–you who will have set the seal upon this whole epoch by the very fact of your having lived in it. I know and you know too that I am not exaggerating. How the educated man of today envies the contemporaries of Socrates and Plato; and yet in the figure of Socrates, Plato is only recording the change of consciousness that had taken place long before, the final liberation of man from associative thought, and the final establishment of causal-logical thinking. But you have won all alone the battle for analytic thought; in your single person you have combined the conqueror of this whole territory together with its explorer and cartographer; you have restored associative thought to man by incorporating it in causal-logical thought, without depriving it of its own character and by turning it into a therapeutic force for the diseased psyche. This is more than the achievement of Plato and his Socrates and it is inevitable that it should be so, for in you the logos of the West and the age-old current of knowledge from the East have been wrought into a unity. It is this unity which created analysis and it is analysis which can bring about the slow unshackling of mankind. That is how it is: you have got to bear with me while I say it and I cannot change the facts.

The treatment of my eye is progressing satisfactorily. The vision of my right eye has improved considerably and that of my left will certainly be improved. However, even this optical diathermy cannot work miracles and my chief weapon for dealing with my ailment remains patience. Naturally, the credulous element within me had a profound trust in the doctor's enthusiasm and I believed that the drop of liquid in my right eye would dry up without further trouble. But that is not happening and I am biting back my disappointment. . . .[1]

Wednesday, 14. I have just started to have Jacob Bernays' book read aloud to me. We are, however, still at the introduction which contains much new information and presents Nietzsche's teacher Ritschl[2] in a new light. Bernays himself is very clear and I understand a great deal of it because I once met one of his grandsons or some other descendant of his in Husserl's[3] seminar. I can imagine just what he looked like physically. I am taking the book with me to the mountains, so that I can read it when the children and my assistant, Lily, are skiing. My dear little wife has just gone to Paris to learn to paint, or more accurately, to liberate the painter within her. She writes very happily. Are you all right again? Before my revision of *Caliban* I am going to read *Group Psychology and the Analysis of the Ego*[4] and I am looking forward to it. How glad I am to be your faithful pupil.

A. Zweig

I am a little nervous of the analogy with Paul Heyse.

[1] Punctuation as in original.

[2] Friedrich W. Ritschl (1816–76): Professor of Classical Philology in Halle, Breslau, Bonn.

[3] Edmund Husserl (1859–1938): Professor of Philosophy in Göttingen and Freiburg.

[4] S. Freud: *Group Psychology and the Analysis of the Ego. St. Ed.* XVIII, pp. 67 ff.

Dear Father Freud,

I feel I must write and wish you a Happy New Year. With each new essay I read you help me forwards and upwards out of the confusions which as reanimated unconscious residues oppress and overshadow me. These residues took from me my pleasure in life, work and success and distorted my relationship to my wife and children and prevented my sleeping, because I knew that by means of your methods and your inspired step-by-step approach it would be possible to get at what was unresolved within me, and yet I knew of no access to the magic formulas. After reading 'Metapsychology of Dreams'[1] and 'Mourning and Melancholia'[2] I saw the light, I dreamt an excellent dream and I feel that I am on the right path. And yet I had only brought the book here with me for the sake of *Group Psychology and the Analysis of the Ego* to help me with my revision of *Caliban*.

And at the same time you have afforded me help of a scientific nature which acted like a flash of lightning for me when I was describing a case of amentia[3]: the hero of my next novel, whose psychical transformations I have had clear in my mind for a year now, goes through a state of mind which I have experienced completely myself, and which you have helped me to understand scientifically. So thank you for everything and may you have lovely bright days in January, such as we are enjoying here in December. I am coming to Vienna in February – I shall fix the dates while I am here and I will write to you soon.

Till then, a good 1933.

Yours
Zweig

[1] S. Freud: 'Metapsychological Supplement to the Theory of Dreams', *St. Ed.* XIV, pp. 222 ff.

[2] S. Freud: 'Mourning and Melancholia', *St. Ed.* XIV, pp. 237 ff.

[3] Amentia: Extreme form of psychosis, combined with hallucinations, delusions and loss of orientation.

Dear Meister Arnold,

A pleasure to hear from you. Probably you cannot yet decide when to follow your wife and children to the Holy Land.

I am fit to work once again but I cannot climb my stairs, am therefore under house arrest. I think this time I have established my right to a sudden fatal heart attack, not a bad prospect. It was a coronary thrombosis; however, I am still alive and as I do not smoke any more I am hardly likely to write anything again—except letters. It reminds me of that Chasen[1] of whom it was said: he'll live, but he won't sing. I have no friends in Paris, only pupils. My favourite and the most interesting, Princess George of Greece (Marie Bonaparte), is in Denmark at the moment. Of the others I might mention Dr. Laforgue and Dr. R. Löwenstein (formerly of Berlin). But I have a son in Paris—Oliver,[2] who with wife and child lives in 16me, 36 rue George Sand. He is a civil engineer, a very talented man, knows everything, excellent at his job; nice wife and charming little daughter. I'm afraid he will not achieve anything in Paris. I'd be very pleased if you could meet him. I will send him your address. I like thinking of you both together.

Ever yours
Freud

On board the Mariette Pasha
16. xii. 33

Dear Father Freud,

My last lines from Europe are to you. I have had an unusually exhausting time and I have had to leave my ms. behind not quite ready for the printers. But Dita[3] begged

---

[1] Chasen: Hebrew for the precentor in the synagogue.
[2] Oliver Freud, born 1891, Freud's second son.   [3] A. Zweig's wife.

me to come when she was not well, and now that she is better again I cannot go back.

I had two long talks with Oliver. I'll write more from Tel Aviv. My address there is Beth Svorai. From Jan. 1st in Haifa: Mount Carmel, Pension Wollstein.

To a happy meeting in the coming year!

Your faithful
Arnold Zweig

Haifa, Mount Carmel, Wollstein House
Palestine
21. i. 34

Dear Father Freud,

In the centre of Haifa, smoking my last French cigar, at last I can settle down to write to you. I just cannot tell you how many mornings I have longed to get in touch with you by means of pen and paper, but every time some irritation of the daily round has prevented me. At one moment the central heating did not function, at another the oil stove was smelling, at another the rain was coming in through the door and I had to stop it up. Then the wind changed, the rain came in through the window, and it took a lot of patience, time, cunning and newspaper before one could hold a match near the closed window without its being blown out. At the moment Carmel is an impressive, desolate landscape, almost Scottish; situated between the bay and the open sea, it is full of pines, stones and puddles of rain, and above it the grey, wind-swept sky is occasionally broken by sunshine. We are living, not in barracks, as you might perhaps imagine, but in the most modern hotel up here; central heating means that it is Order of the Eagle, first class, black, with oak leaves and swords.[1] But the engineer who installed the central heating left the builder out of his reckoning and he forgot the chimney. When this was added later it was too narrow, and

[1] The highest German military decoration.

55

now, in the middle of the rainy weather, it has had to be widened and replaced by another. And even now the wind that whines and howls round the hotel seldom permits the heating to function properly.

You will find, dear Father Freud, that I am expatiating too much upon the central heating, but these questions of practical life, where the apparatus of civilisation functions only creakingly, are the main problems in this country. We are not prepared to give up our standard of living and this country is not yet prepared to satisfy it. And since the Palestinian Jews are rightly proud of what does exist and since we are rightly irritated about what does not, there is much friction on the quiet, especially among the women, much vexation about the immense expense of effort these trifles demand. So far I have not done a stroke of work, apart from reading the proofs of the *Bilanz der deutschen Judenheit*.[1] Dita and I are living in one room; another unheated room has been put at Dita's disposal as an atelier and here Lily and I often write our letters as well. You will doubtless remember Lily Offenstadt. She is now married to a young friend of mine and her name is now Lily Leuchter-Offenstadt.

She and her husband have come out here so that she can continue to work for me. Her husband, one of the chief electrical engineers in Bewag, was thrown out of his job on April 1st, despite the fact that he had served at the front for two years with the infantry and later in the Reichswehr. He was too decent to have any truck with the Nazis. Now he'll be able to get a new job here under favourable auspices.

You will doubtless guess that while I was dictating these last few sentences my thoughts were with your son, Oliver. From Bandol or perhaps indeed from aboard ship I sent you the last letter I wrote from Europe. And since I've been here I have been thinking very much about this son of yours, who is also too decent to find it easy to adapt himself to life.

[1] English translation: *Insulted and Exiled. The Truth about the German Jews*. John Miles, 1937.

It was shattering to observe how he too talked most vividly and warmly when speaking about his wartime service. Just like all other men of his generation and of his circumstances who now find that they have to begin all over again at a time when they are firmly set in their ways of thought and feeling, habits and ambitions. No one can take it amiss if these men do not wish to have anything to do with the contemporary business scene and prefer to take refuge in memories of a time when a man (especially a young man) merely needed to risk his life to be fulfilling all the demands that society made upon him.

I think of you full of curiosity to know how you have survived this winter of our discontent. In my book *Bilanz* I have written about you in almost too many places, quite apart from an essay of some eight to ten pages in the middle of the book, where I had to outline the importance of analysis and the significance of your personality. As soon as I have the proofs of this section I will send them to you. Perhaps people will sense that they contain a minute extract of the admiration, gratitude and love that I and not only I feel towards you.

I am unusually well, to give you some quick news about myself. All the depressions which have often tortured me so terribly in recent years have vanished. The Fatherland, the Father State, the economic burden, concern about the preservation of my property—all this has dropped away from me and with it have gone many tensions and compulsive ideas. I don't care any more about 'the land of my fathers'. I haven't got any more Zionistic illusions either. I view the necessity of living here among the Jews without enthusiasm, without any false hopes and even without the desire to scoff. I am grateful for the stroke of fate which united us as young people with this remarkable phenomenon here and which forced us to come here for the sake of our children and our young friends. But Dita and I are just as much, or as little, emigrants here as we were in the South of France. The affinity between the two regions and the easygoing nature of life in the two places have marvellously facilitated the transition from one to the other, and the landscape which surrounds us here appeals to us just as much as Provence or the Wienerwald. I am sure that things will settle down all right and that we will establish a happy relationship with the country and its inhabitants and that we will grow to appreciate the many fine and charming people that we find here. Our faith in the use of reason in human life cannot be destroyed, either, by this terrible return to barbarism, just because we were wrong in our calculations about time and thought we were living in the modern age, whereas in the execution of poor van der Lubbe[1] we see the return to the Middle Ages. Our brave and sensible children in their children's hostel and children's village community respectively make it easy for us to adapt ourselves here. It is just my enthusiasm, founded as it was on a pleasant illusion, that is gone and I do not shed a tear at its departure. More about this another time; first I would like to send you my *Bilanz*. Unfortunately it cannot appear before the end of February and I hope to hear from you before then. Kind regards to you all, especially to your wife and yourself, and I hope the ignominy of Austria leaves you more indifferent than you were six months ago, and that in spite of everything you find consolation in the importance of your work for the fact that even you are forced to waste your substance in this, the most stupid of all epochs.

Ever your faithful
Arnold Zweig

[1] Marinus van der Lubbe: Accused and convicted of setting fire to the Reichstag in Berlin in 1933; guillotined 1934.

Dear Meister Arnold,

I have long waited eagerly for your letter, so that I might reply, and I am delighted with it now that it has come, moving as it does from the central heating to the central problems of integration, from my son Oliver to your *Bilanz*. First of all about the last mentioned. I am eager to read it, now that I know you are cured of your unhappy love of your so-called Fatherland. Such a passion is not for the likes of us. I'm afraid that under the influence of our personal relationship you have talked too much about me in your book, and that would be harmful to you and of no use to me, for let us make no mistake, this day and age has rejected me and all I had to give, and acclamations will not cause it to revise its judgement. Probably my time will come but, I might add, for the moment it is past.

A few months ago I had an unpleasant experience with a journalist, an echo of which may come to your ears. That's why I am writing to you about it. Last October there visited me a Dr. Ludwig Bauer who was known to me from some unusually intelligent and perceptive articles on the political situation. When I learnt that he was Viennese, the son of a doctor, a friend of Arthur Schnitzler and Beer-Hofmann,[1] I treated him as a friend and discussed the dangers and prospects of our situation with him. Fool that I was! A few weeks later the fellow published an article on Austria in several newspapers, reporting also his visit to me. He described how I, good old man that I am, highly regarded and helpless, trembling with fear, had seized him by both hands and had kept on repeating just the one question: 'Do you think they will turn me out, do you think they will take my books away?' I heard of this appeal to the sympathy of Europe through a letter to my daughter Anna from the Zurich

[1] Richard Beer-Hofmann (1866–1935): Austrian lyric poet and playwright.

psychiatrist Maier,[1] in which he asked if it would comfort me in my depression to know that I could find asylum in Burghölzli[2] at any time. Naturally what Bauer had written was all an impertinent fabrication. With the disregard for truth peculiar to journalists he had worked me up into a sensation. When I protested bitterly to him he flared up and expected me to be grateful because he had proclaimed my importance to 'millions of readers', which had earned him the reproach of having much overestimated me. I still have a nasty taste in my mouth from this encounter and he is supposed to be on our side!

The worst thing about old age is the increasing feeling of helplessness. I read most of your *Spielzeug*[3] but much of it seemed to me to break off prematurely. Naturally what I found most deeply moving was the piece you created out of your own eye trouble. I hope you realise that you still have a large public even though you have few purchasers. I am not working any more; my organs don't cooperate properly and it is hard enough to squeeze the five hours daily of analysis out of the old organism. One must not always go on working indefinitely. Something began to take shape not long ago but it slipped away again. Had you been here we could have talked about it.

Kind regards to you, your wife and to Lily O.-L.

Ever yours
Freud

Haifa, Mount Carmel, Wollstein House
10. ii. 34

Dear Father Freud,

Your long letter delighted and comforted me in spite of the unwelcome things you were obliged to report. I say

[1] Hans Maier: Swiss psychiatrist.
[2] Cantonal mental asylum; formerly under the direction of Bleuler and Jung.
[3] English translation: *Playthings of Time*. Martin Secker, 1935.

delighted, because in the passionate intensity of your response, as it is reflected in your handwriting, there is comfort and confirmation for me of my own explosive temperament, which is always ready to erupt, and I am comforted because the superiority of your mind is never revealed more clearly than when you tell of things that have infuriated you, and with justification. This Dr. Ludwig Bauer certainly has the reputation of being one of the best journalists writing in German today; I heard his collected essays much praised while I was at Sanary. I have not read any of his books, but I know them by name and I had always wanted to remedy this. He used to sit in a café in Sanary, a bloated lump with a beard–I never wanted to make his acquaintance. And now you remove the last of the illusions I had about him–and now let us be done with him.

The worst thing about our anti-Nazi journals seems to me to be that one cannot rely on any one of the contributors' being a really strong character. They would be much better if they were not written by hypertrophied intellectuals, but had instead something of the 'fairness' of English journalism. They always remind me somewhat of a harem with pretty women all carrying on intrigues. Carl von Ossietzky's[1] special position in German journalism was founded on his integrity. And now we shall not read a line more of his either.

And now you too are going to leave us in the lurch as a writer? You have every right to do so. Your collected opus represents in my opinion the greatest extension of human knowledge ever accorded us on the most important subject of all, i.e. the subject of our own mental and psychic life. You know, too, that I consider you the culmination of Austrian literature, whose raison d'être has always resided in its mastery of psychological analysis. Only you are far more than that, as you know. I do not want to plagiarise myself, but it is your terrestrial significance which must surely give

[1] Carl von Ossietzky (1889–1938): Editor of *Die Weltbühne*. Awarded Nobel Peace Prize 1934; died in concentration camp.

you the certainty that people will return to you. I should think so, indeed! But if you maintain that you count for little at the moment, the reason is as follows: Freud *and* Tyranny together—impossible. Either one follows your profound teachings and doctrines, controls one's emotions, adapts them to serve as positive forces in the world and then one must fight for the liberation of man and the dethronement of national states, which are only substitute-formations for the Father-Moloch. Or one must perpetuate this Father-Moloch and impose upon mankind as ideal for the future his gradual suppression in a fascist system; if we do this, then analysis and all criticism of the status quo must retreat into the shadows—and you with it. But unfortunately or, rather, thank God, these people miscalculate. The periods of reaction in Europe have always been of long duration; they have always been fundamentally stupid, bloody and crude (though none of them remotely approaches ours in these respects, since none has followed upon so savage an unharnessing of mass passions), but in the long run they have never succeeded in checking or preventing a single creative spirit from exerting its influence.

Through the negligence of my friends and through my own folly I have lost my entire library, which is now waiting in the warehouse in 37 cases to be auctioned by the Nazis. But now when I travel in my mind along my bookshelves, I find every creative critic of man still at work—Isaiah and Socrates, Cervantes and Swift, Voltaire and Heine. So even though you are being thrust into the background in many lands for the moment—they will not stop Sigmund Freud from carrying on his work. It is only sad that the French, who are the most progressive element in the world today, are prevented for the time being by their own repressions, their Chinese-like isolation and their national vanity from recognising the significance, scale and scope of your achievement.[1] I could

[1] The attitude of the French towards psychoanalysis has changed considerably in the meantime.

wish that the chapter on you in my *Bilanz* would give them cause to examine the truth of my statements. Then perhaps an inspired Frenchman would emerge to discover Sigmund Freud. The lack of understanding, even in Jewish-Russian circles, which I met among highly cultured Parisians, amazed me. They are as reactionary in everything as they are in their theatre, where they try to approximate to the German stage of 1910 or to a talented pupil of the Darmstadt Hoftheater. If all goes well I shall be appearing as a revolutionary force on this stage at the end of February or the beginning of March with the play of Sergeant Grischa. My momentary depression has been easily dispelled by the comic side of this situation.

And now I've told you a lot about yourself and nothing at all about myself and yet I know you would prefer it the other way round. I am in a strange state. To put it botanically, I am a late flowerer. I always need six months longer than anyone else, as you know, to understand a subject, but then I understand it properly. And so now I am suffering badly from the depression and melancholy of being uprooted and robbed. I am still living with Dita in a little hotel room; in my work I restrict myself to such an extent that I have just one table to meet all my needs, so I cannot spread out my manuscripts and begin serious work. In between whiles, I am quite calm and happy, but I am suffering under too much self-criticism, which is, as it were, bursting from every pore of my body; and I find it very difficult to get rid of all the dreams of hatred and revenge with which I try to restore my physical equilibrium before going to sleep. I do not like the world just now, dear Father Freud, and I am still a bad enough boy to smash it to smithereens, or at any rate to want to do so. I am bold enough, it is true, to try to reconstruct a little corner of it in a more reasonable and meaningful way in my novel, *Erziehung vor Verdun*, in which I intend to have a thoroughgoing reckoning with the Germans and Nazis. But it will be difficult for me to give the story the same degree of simplicity and naturalness that I managed in the *Sergeant* and that is what I want to achieve again. I am also doubtful, to be sure, whether I will be able to regard my hero Bertin with as kindly eyes as I did the Sergeant. Indeed in some essential points I am still far from the clarity I require to make a start. Without repeating myself it is hard to describe all over again the confrontation between a man and the vicious, mean world around him which has grown as rigid as a machine, and to describe it in such a way that an organically constructed piece of human life becomes the backbone of the story. And to strike the happy mean and see the autobiographical element in the same way as the rest of the material in the book (and also not more artificially), to treat the hero neither too leniently nor too harshly—all this is going to be quite a job. Another time I'll describe to you the landscape where this battle of a writer with his own past and his present work is taking place. Today I have only to convey the thanks and greetings of the two industrious women who are both at work in this room, one of them drawing, the other typing. And I take your hands (as you took Herr Bauer's), i.e. in my imagination, and rejoice that we are contemporaries.

With warmest greetings to all

Ever your

Zweig

Vienna IX, Berggasse 19

25. ii. 34

Dear Meister Arnold,

Work hard at the *Erziehung vor Verdun*, put into it all the sarcasm, cruelty and feeling of superiority that these recent months have produced within you; firstly because I am longing to read the book—best of all in the shade of a garden with Wolf[1] and Jofi[2] in the grass beside me—and I cannot

---

[1] Anna Freud's Alsatian.   [2] S. Freud's chow.

be sure how much more time I have. And secondly, because to my mind the people who should read your book are already shifting their interest from the war and the past to concentrate it exclusively upon the incredibly astonishing events to be expected in the immediate future. So see to it that you are not too late.

Our little bit of civil war was not at all nice.[1] You could not go out without your passport, electricity was cut off for a day, and the thought that the water supply might run out was very unpleasant. Now everything is calm, the calm of tension, you might say; just like waiting in a hotel room for the second shoe to be flung against the wall. It cannot go on like this; something is bound to happen. Whether the Nazis will come, or whether our own home-made Fascism will be ready in time, or whether Otto von Habsburg will step in, as people now think. I have a story in the back of my mind which I cannot remember exactly; it's called 'The Lady and the Tiger' and in it a poor prisoner is waiting in a circus, not knowing whether they are going to let the wild beast loose upon him or whether the lady will appear who by choosing him for her husband will release him from punishment. The point of the story is that it ends without our knowing who has arrived, the lady or the tiger. This can only mean that for the prisoner it does not matter which has happened and that it is not worth telling us.

You are quite right in your expectation that we intend to stick it out here resignedly. For where should I go in my state of dependence and physical helplessness? And everywhere abroad is so inhospitable. Only if there really were a satrap of Hitler's ruling in Vienna I would no doubt have to go, no matter where. My attitude to the parties who are quarrelling with one another I can only describe by plagiarising Shakespeare's Mercutio–'A plague on both your houses.'

[1] The conflict between Chancellor Dollfuss and the Heimwehr against the Socialists.

We were all very sorry to hear that the Nazis are in possession of your fine library. My daughter Anna has the following
idea: have you not got an urgent desire to possess right away
as a substitute for what you have lost a collected edition of
my writings, which you seem to esteem so highly? If you confess to this wish, when and where may the Verlag send these
eleven volumes? And please don't thank me, I would never
have had so kind a thought. But it cannot have remained
concealed from you that fate has granted me as compensation
for much that has been denied me the possession of a daughter
who, in tragic circumstances, would not have fallen short of
Antigone.

Write again soon and tell me what you and the two busy
ladies are doing. How long can you stay on Mt. Carmel?
Probably for the whole summer.

Ever yours
Freud

Vienna, 21. iii. 34

Did my letter of 26. ii. not reach you?

Ever yours Fr.

Carmel, Haifa
23. iii. 34

Dear Father Freud,

Your last letter, eagerly awaited, arrived here during my
absence. I was driving round the country with Dita, as this
time of year is so suitable for touring and the country is so
beautiful now. The letter reached me in Tiberias, where I
met Lily. I don't know where to begin with my reply. First
of all, I am delighted that you could and still can write so
freely. We do not need to tell one another that the destructive
instinct is stronger everywhere today than the constructive.
So why should things be different in Vienna? Are we going

to admit or try to establish differences of degree? Must we give vent to lamentations about all this? Ever since 1914 we have had bleeding human bodies before our eyes and every scab that forms is scratched off again. If Austria were to be the last of our sadistic experiences we should be lucky. But our fated generation certainly will not get off as lightly as that. I still have hope that Europe will not be destroyed, for hope seems to be a by-product of well-functioning glands. But belief? I've long given up belief. *Qui vivra, verra*—there is no more to be said. And the fact that you are at work, unbowed and unchanging, gives me so much pleasure that I am prepared to accept without protest all the insidious changes that have taken place in the Vienna I know.

I accept with gratitude the wonderful joy which you and your daughter are bestowing on me in the shape of a work which is unrivalled in our time. Yesterday or the day before I sent you a packet of printed matter containing the pages of *Bilanz* which touch upon your work and its practical consequences. I shall never tire of reading you and seeing your findings confirmed. I have to restrict the amount of time I spend reading on account of my eyes, and since I have all too much firsthand experience of the devastating effects of neurosis and of the extraordinary compensation formations it gives rise to, and since I also have an eye for spotting its effects in other human beings, I look forward to reading and re-reading your works for the next few years. I did possess early Deuticke editions of your most important works—*The Interpretation of Dreams, Three Essays, Psycho-Pathology of Everyday Life, Totem and Taboo* and (apart from other collections) the new collections of the Psychoanalytischer Verlag. But now at last I shall be able to read them properly for myself or get someone to read to me from the eleven folios. Your Anna! Please give her my warmest thanks and greetings. I was always sorry that she was so busy that I could never have a talk with her about her work as I was able to with you. But I hope to put that right one day. Where it will be done, the future will show. Once my novel is finished I shall go to Europe to get it published. And while the publisher is reading it I shall be able to travel around, and so I could go to Vienna, if that suited you, or to wherever else you might be. Once the printing begins, I don't want to be too far from Holland. That would mean a saving of four weeks in time.

My work has started and looks quite hopeful. I had to overcome great inner difficulties. I could not identify myself any more with my former ego and I could not summon up the proper positive feelings towards my hero, Bertin. But in my critical attitude towards him I could not get a proper hold on him, either. So it was very difficult to get the story moving on a proper keel, to sift all the material and to retain just the central points, and to use the action to weld them together with a feeling of inevitability. And the basic problem is such an important one – the cultured man who refuses to recognise reality and who would like to cling to his childhood in the shape of the war! He has fallen into a den of murderers which he regards and insists on regarding as a den of noble knights – coûte que coûte. He is then slowly moulded into shape by the sheer mechanical passage of time till he is forced to concede: Yes, the world is as it is; the Germans are as they are; and my ego is as I am. Well, you will see. Ever since 1928 I have been turning and twisting the material around, but now I've got it. And since I take the war merely as an example of human society at its most intense and treat it quite concretely, I hope a readable book will be in our hands before the beginning of the winter. If only you will take care of yourself till then and protect yourself against all the iniquities of our age.

Next time I'll tell you all about my loved ones (and my tormentors!) here. But for today just warmest greetings from our family to yours; salutations to your Anna-Antigone, and to you my best and dearest wishes.

Yours
Zweig

68

Delighted at your acceptance; but to be on the safe side let me know where the eleven should be sent.

Easter greetings.

Yours

F.

Carmel, Haifa
2. iv. 34

Dear Father Freud,

When your kind card of enquiry arrived I was just about to get myself photographed, so that I could at last send you a decent picture of myself. For a moment I was afraid that my letter and the proof sheets of *Bilanz* which I had sent off previously had not reached you. Then I remembered Time and Space, which are usually the province of our good fellow warrior Einstein, and I plucked up hope again. This letter, if I send it by air, will reach you in less than a week (fortunately one never takes into account all that can happen in a week). The photo may perhaps take longer, if the plane does not accept large packets as business or ordinary letters. So should this letter arrive by itself, it is just an advance guard.

My work has got off to a good start, and the splenetic nature I am developing, which will enable me to be as unjust as I like to all the accursed interruptions which have beset me since last March, will stand the book in good stead. It will be a faithful picture of human nature that I'm planning, not without humour in the situation, and as I see wherever I look the hated face of the Triumvirate Hi-Goe-Goe,[1] and also showing through some of my own characters, the Nazis and the spineless Germans in the army will not come off too well, as you can imagine. The most difficult thing to do was to bring the vital elements of fate into this

[1] Hitler, Göring, Goebbels.

novel, which is really a sociological novel, for it is these elements alone which lend dimension and distance to the whole–that, namely, which plays its part outside the various individual personalities. I am not satisfied about this point so far. There still remains a lot of work to be done and great is the temptation to be lazy. For the sea looks close at hand, but by car it is quite a distance away, and if one wants to bathe one has to sacrifice three valuable hours to do so.

Farewell. I am so much looking forward to getting your works.

With kindest regards and good wishes from my family to yours.

Yours
Zweig

Vienna IX, Berggasse 19
3. iv. 34

Dear Meister Arnold,

The old story has it that when the 10,000 led by Xenophon after a long march through Asia Minor finally reached the coast and beheld the sea, they shouted in amazement: θαλασσα, θαλασσα. Xenophon who was standing near remarked: 'One can also say θαλαττα.'

On p. 232 of your *Bilanz* please correct Subconscious to Unconscious and on p. 234 Ferency to Ferenczi.

Ever yours
Freud

P.S. Oh, also *Edward* Jones on p. 254 to *Ernest* J.

Vienna IX, Berggasse 19
4. 4. 34

Postscript to my letter of yesterday.

As soon as I had sent off my letter it occurred to me that I had made a mistake in it and that I had written θαλασσα with a second λ. As far as I can judge it must have been a slip against my better knowledge.[1] But I soon understood its motivation. I had been irritated by the little inaccuracies in your essay. I am always very touchy about little things.

(Ferency, Edward Jones, Subconscious): instead of telling you this outright, I quoted the anecdote from Xenophon. But love intervened and said: Probably you are not to blame for these little errors. It's not as easy for you as for others to correct your proofs. The Subconscious may well have been the result of your secretary's not hearing you correctly, and anyway I don't like criticising you. You shall therefore receive atonement and the best atonement is to make a little error oneself, which you will notice and charge me with. That is how the θαλλαττα arose and this is the explanation for it. Besides I have always been proud of how much Greek I have remembered (choruses from Sophocles, passages from Homer).

Ever yours
Freud

Carmel
6. iv. 34

Dear Father Freud,

Thank you for your second card and for the approaching eleven. I am looking forward to them tremendously, just like a schoolboy.

Meanwhile I have sent you

(1) Printed matter, including galleys of *Bilanz*.
(2) A letter written by hand.
(3) A far too large photograph.

Has everything arrived? By the same post I sent the Verlag my exact address. Your handwriting shows me that you are in good fettle. Has spring arrived with you and do you drive out into the country now and then? Give my regards to

[1] Actually, Freud had not made a slip but spelled the word correctly.

Anna and her friend, who will doubtless be taking you with them to Hochroterd once the catkins are out. My work is going well.

But I ought to be split in two, so that the one AZ could go over and polish up what the other AZ has dictated.

Here mimosa, lemons and innumerable mountain flowers are in bloom.

All the best wishes to all of you from all of us.

Yours
Zweig

Vienna
15. 4. 34

Photo received; framed; put into place.　　　Yours Fr.

Haifa
23. iv. 34

Dear Father Freud,

The eleven are now here, and already I see a twelfth on the horizon to bring the number up to that of the apostles and the months of the year. I was delighted, as is and was my wont – a quiet deep delight. And I was happier than I have been since last March. The personal bond between you and me has, as it were, acquired concrete form through this splendid gift: the foundation stone of a library as well as of life. Please tell Anna once again how much this kindness means to me. I shall soon appear in person to thank her myself. I made straight for the Leonardo essay[1] and I am now deep in it. The splendid large print helps to save my eyes. But this little essay is as exciting as a short story and shows such finesse and care in its interpretation that one can only approve and nod one's head in admiration. And that

[1] S. Freud: *Leonardo da Vinci and a memory of his childhood. St. Ed.* XI, pp. 63 ff.

you should interpret the little *slip* in your one letter so quickly in the next and in the way you did – that is a truly charming and fatherly gesture. And, moreover, I am in no way responsible for correcting the proofs of that book. I had it read in Paris, so that it might appear more quickly, and that has all taken *so* long!

Dear Father Freud, I am taking up my analysis again. I just cannot shake off the whole Hitler business. My affect has shifted to someone who looked after our affairs for us in 1933 under difficulties. But this affect of mine is an obsession. I don't live in the present, but am 'absent'. My work grows shapeless, insipid and shallow and my imagination, instead of going into the characters, expresses itself compulsively in sadistic wish-phantasies about war. Dr. S. is here and tomorrow I shall begin. Perhaps he will succeed in overcoming my amnesia about my childhood and getting at the source of these disturbances. And then I shall be able to be truly happy and enjoy the wonderful cool sunny weather of Mt. Carmel.

What are your plans? You will get *Bilanz* from Holland.

Ever yours
Arnold Zweig

Haifa
24. iv. 34

Dear Father Freud,

Your card[1] arrived delightfully in the middle of my intention to send you a letter with corrections, such as you sent me after your Thalatta mistake! Dita has pointed out that I must already have read the Leonardo essay *twice* – once in about 1911 and once after the war. This time her memory was the more accurate and mine, which is usually very good, had simply no trace of having read it. The reason is quite clear: the essay fits me too perfectly. One of my situations

[1] See Freud's card of 15. 4. 34.

73

must have run closely parallel with the one described here with such genius, and so my repression felt itself threatened and hurt, and since vengeance is sweet it repressed what was calculated to remove it. Dita reminded me of how we had reacted then, when we did not yet understand anything about it. In a week we are moving into our flat—'alles neu macht der Mai'.[1] If only my photo were a sound photo, just as there are now sound films, so that it could give you a birthday greeting!

Ever yours
Zweig

Haifa, Carmel
28. 4. 34

Dear Father Freud,

This is to reach you on May 6th and congratulate you with a bow and a kiss on the hand, as grandchildren used to do in days gone by. And so that it may not come empty-handed it brings with it the first draft of a plan that I would like to start on as soon as the *Erziehung* is finished: i.e. a novel about Nietzsche's madness. You know that ever since the end of the war I have turned away bitterly from this idol of my youth. There are signs of this in several of my books, clearest of all in *Bilanz*. Now after many years I have come close to him again, because in you I recognized the man who has carried out all that Nietzsche first dreamt of: who has given new life to the world of antiquity, who has reversed old values, who has made a clean sweep of Christianity, who is the true immoralist and a-theist; who has given new names to the human instincts and who has contributed a critique of the course of civilization as we know it—and whatever else there was in common between you. But you have avoided all his distortions and follies, just because you invented analysis and not Zarathustra.

[1] 'All made new by the month of May', from a German folk song.

At Dr. S.'s I came upon a book by Podach,[1] which I am now slowly consuming and imbibing, so that later I can embark on the creative process. I want to describe F. Nietzsche the man, at the height of his happiness in Turin; I want to describe his blissful lack of inhibition in writing, his timidity, his charm, his joy in little things. Beyond the horizon loom the Goat, his sister, politely known as the Llama, and Frau Pastor Nietzsche; the Father who died at 35, and Jacob Burckhardt[2] who had rightly dropped him; but in the sky, veiled in clouds is the constellation of Ariadne (Cosima[3] and Lou, the woman from afar, the Non-Goatlike, the sublime Feminine, the intellectual Eros). Then comes the breakdown: the release from convulsive tension, struggle and reality, when the conflict between family and ego is no longer bearable, and the flight into the new worlds of the Crucified and Dionysus. Then I shall give in double and triple focus what takes place in reality (R), what the mother (M) realises of this and what F. N. himself experiences,

so that his truly pitiful fate is fulfilled; when the gates of Hades, of the family, close behind him. I would like to develop the healthy bourgeois figure of his friend Overbeck[4] as the antagonist to the Goat, Lisbeth; also to round out the figure of Jacob Burckhardt and to introduce a further dozen people, but always laying the emphasis on the world of delusion and expanding that fully. It is just the plot that still worries me. For neither a case history nor the portrayal of a delusion is a plot, whatever Th. Mann may think, and I still do not see my way clearly. But if you or even perhaps Frau Lou would be interested in helping me, then I'd be able to produce a

---

[1] Erich T. Podach: *Gestalten um Nietzsche*. Weimar, 1932.

[2] Jacob Burckhardt (1818–97): Swiss historian of art and culture.

[3] Cosima Wagner (1837–1930): Liszt's daughter; married Richard Wagner.

[4] Franz Overbeck (1837–1905): Professor of Theology in Basel.

Counter-Grischa. And your name would stand on the dedicatory page.

Ever yours
Zweig

That you should have framed my photo and given it a place makes me very happy. Thank you very much.

Vienna XIX, Strassergasse 41
11. v. 34

Dear Meister Arnold,

No greeting on my 78th birthday has preoccupied me more closely than yours. I would like best to go on thinking about my reply for another week, but what would you be thinking of me by that time? So I shall begin today and continue in the next few days.

I do not—as yet—know the book by Podach that has so fired you. I shall read it through if you would like me to. I am enclosing the crazy announcement of a book by a probably imperfectly cured psychotic, who claims to have penetrated the mystery of Friedrich Nietzsche. You can never tell what such a fool may not have puzzled out for himself. Our friend Lou is over 70 years old and as far as I can judge from this distance, not in the best of health. She never writes about herself in her letters and she never complains. She must be one of the few people alive who know anything intimate about him. And she is not given to telling it. Certainly she would only do so by word of mouth. She never wanted to tell me about him. For your purposes she would of course be invaluable. All these are just superficial comments.

12. v. 34

The first Iceman,[1] but a glorious summer day; the garden in front of my window is truly a place in which 'to die in

---

[1] The saints whose feast days fall on May 12, 13, 14 are known as the Icemen in the German-speaking countries, as these days are traditionally cold.

beauty'. I am wondering whether I should advise for or against the execution of your plan. I am much more clearly conscious of my inclinations against the project than the reasons for it. But no doubt it will not matter what I say. The poetic urge, if it's strong enough, will prove itself stronger.

It seems to me that we touch here on the problem of poetic licence versus historical truth. I know my feelings on this point are thoroughly conservative. Where there is an unbridgeable gap in history and biography, the writer can step in and try to guess how it all happened. In an uninhabited country he may be allowed to establish the creatures of his imagination. Even when the historical facts are known but sufficiently remote and removed from common knowledge, he can disregard them. Thus it cannot be held against Shakespeare that in about the year 1000 Macbeth was a just and benevolent king of Scotland. But on the other hand, where reality is firmly established and has become common property, the writer should respect it. When B. Shaw makes his Caesar stand and gape at a stony Sphinx just as though he were a Cook's tourist and forget to take leave of Cleopatra when he leaves Egypt, he proves to us what a clown he is and that a joke means more to him than anything. The historical Caesar summoned Cleopatra to Rome after the birth of her son Caesarion and there she remained till her flight after Caesar's murder. It's true, the poets usually fail to keep these rules, e.g. Schiller in *Don Carlos*, Goethe in *Egmont* and *Goetz* etc., but it's frequently not an advantage when they do fail to do so.

Now when it is a question of someone so near to us in time and whose influence is still as active as Friedrich Nietzsche's, a description of his character and his destiny should aim at the same result as a portrait does – that is to say, however the conception may be elaborated the main stress should fall on the resemblance. And since the subject cannot sit for the portrait, one has first to collect so much

material about him that it only needs to be supplemented
with a sympathetic understanding. Otherwise we will be
faced with what happened to the devoted son and the
Hungarian painter: 'Poor Father, how much you have
changed!' And just think, what would we do with this
imaginary Friedrich Nietzsche? You must know whether
there is enough material available to make such a portrait.
Podach's book appears to have made you certain on this
point, but in the case of Friedrich Nietzsche we are confronted with something else, beyond what is usual. It is the
case history of a sick man, and this is much more difficult
to guess or reconstruct. I mean, there are psychical processes
in a certain sequence but not always psychical motivations
generating them, and in the unravelling of these one could
go very much astray. Anyway if it is a case history, for the
layman the main interest is gone.

I do not know whether these are my real arguments
against your plan. Perhaps the relationship you establish
between Nietzsche and me also plays a part in my reasons.
In my youth he was a remote and noble figure to me. A
friend of mine, Dr. Paneth,[1] had got to know him in the
Engadine and had written a lot to me about him. Later too
my relationship to him was more or less as you describe in
Bilanz. To return to the latter – I found it distressing to read.
I hope it has done you good to write it and that it has en-
abled you to let off steam, for I am almost stifled with suppressed rancour and fury. Of course I do not believe half
what you write about me in *Bilanz*. But all the same my
friend Yvette[2] has a little song in her repertoire: Ça fait
toujours plaisir.

My birthday went off without damage to me, since no
congratulatory visitors were admitted. Flowers are naturally
harmless. We have scarcely ever lived in more beautiful

---

[1] Josef Paneth (1857–90): Student friend of Freud's; see F.'s letter to
Martha Bernays, 15. iv. 1884.
[2] Yvette Guilbert (1866–1943): French *diseuse*.

surroundings than here and seldom have I suffered more. One must just put up with it, since the mechanical aid is so inadequate.

My best wishes for the *Erziehung*.

Ever yours
Freud

Vienna XIX, Strassergasse 47
22. v. 34

Dear Meister Arnold,

It seemed to me that dissuading someone is not the proper behaviour for a friend. So I asked Frau Lou whether her cooperation would be available. I enclose her answer,[1] which please return.

Yours
Freud

Haifa, Carmel, Beth Moses
6. 6. 34

Dear Father Freud,

I have long been meaning to answer your sympathetic letter, but we have been so busy getting our flat ready. Things are making progress in spite of a hundred and one difficulties, and in the middle of it all we had to go to Tel Aviv to visit the Levantine Fair, which is well worth seeing. And now I am back here again, while Dita is still in Tel Aviv, and I have agreed to give a lecture this evening on 'The

---

[1] On 20. 5. 1934, Lou Andreas-Salomé wrote to Freud: 'I wish to lose no time in adding one further point to this short letter of greeting and thanks, since you put the question to me at the end of your letter: it concerns the Nietzsche project. It is absolutely out of the question that I should participate in this in any way. I cannot consider such a thing and the mere thought of it fills me with dismay. Please tell this to your correspondent in the strongest and most final terms—moreover, how right you are to dissuade him altogether from his Nietzsche plan!'

Psychological Consequences of Deracination'. So I am not really in a letter-writing mood. But for the last few days your marvellously paternal second letter, and with it Frau Lou's enclosure, have left me no peace. Nobody who means as much to me as you has ever tried so hard to dissuade me from a plan and never has it been so in vain. You are right in all you say. My opinion about historical truth coincides entirely with yours. I have absolutely no intention of making up, of fabricating or reconstructing a Nietzsche. My aim is to fathom and describe the terrible gap which exists between the character and the writings of a German and to confront the brother Fritz with his sister Lisbeth, with Hitler always looming like a shadow over her. I would like to describe the man's flight and his capture, his soft, gentle timidity and his thunderous words which anticipate the Nazi era. I would like to confront him with Overbeck and I would like to have Jacob Burckhardt sit in judgement on him. I would like to depict his enjoyment of the landscape and to describe the nightmare his contemporaries meant to him. He was never anything but a philologist of genius—among words he was always happy, words satisfied him completely. But, alas, that he should have turned them in such a way that they stirred other people into action—and that is exactly what they did do. I would like to establish a link between present-day Germany and his doctrines; I would like to transfer my rage, hate and contempt into his person and share his flight into psychosis, into the dark realm full of magic laws and the wild residues of the psyche, where he could live completely without conflict after his last contacts with reality (his mother, Langbehn, his evil, foolish sister) were over and done with. So Frau Lou herself shall not appear in the story at all, only her central image, Ariadne, vanquished by reality, Lisbeth, the Nazi. I see nothing but the outlines of the story as yet, nothing more than that, but it attracts me very much. You can judge whether dissuasion is of any avail in such a case. F. N. was a youthful love of mine, admired as a prose writer and as a thinker too, but only as far as *Zarathustra*. The later works roused more and more opposition in me. And I shall read him yet again, very carefully, this late Nietzsche. Certainly anything Frau Lou might say would be of inestimable value; but I would like to describe this man's really last attempt to save his life entirely from his own point of view, from his own yearnings and phantasies, and against this background set the deceptions of Lisbeth, the upbraidings of his mother, the Naumburg stuffiness, which were too much for him. It's true that Frau Lou could be of wonderful help in this, but I do not really need this unique help; she must just read the book when it's ready and judge it then–both she and you.

It is wonderful that you are so well accommodated and that you are enjoying these weeks so much. I hope Jofi and the grandchildren will help to make you happy, quite apart from Anna. I myself am in a strange frame of mind. I am full of resistance to my work. I feel like a hedgehog vis-à-vis my own ego; my novel seems terrible to me, and perhaps everything I have been doing in these last few weeks is wrong, except for my analysis with Dr. S. This I found necessary on account of my intense depressions and out-breaks of hatred, and it seems to be progressing well. Without it the flies and the workmen would have driven me mad. If only the journey to Dr. S. did not take so long–every hour of analysis involves an hour before and after. Perhaps we shall now buy a secondhand car though this may mean depriving our children. Then the sea will not be so far away either. I nearly drowned in it on Saturday, though I am a good swimmer. Ah, dear Father Freud, I wish I could describe to you what a muddled-up creature I am just now. And the amnesia about 'the dreams of my youth' is tough and will not give way. But we will manage somehow. Your genius and the excellent Dr. S. will make a breach in it.

And now I must stop, as I must have a rest before my lecture. Recently I have been reading, by way of a change,

E. Ludwig's *Napoleon* and every sentence in it encourages me—not that his Corsican is anything but a cardboard figure, but because the book is so stupid. Till tomorrow morning then, when this letter must go off.

7. vi. 34. Good morning. I could easily begin another letter right away, so intensely does your presence preoccupy me. But first I will send this one off. It's getting hot with us now, even in the morning. Is the weather good with you? I deny your right to say that you are overestimated in *Bilanz*, dear Father Freud. I have probably forgotten some aspects of your work and I have said nothing at all about your personality.

So—I will send Frau Lou's letter back next time; for today warmest greetings from our family to yours.

Yours
Zweig

Haifa, Mount Carmel, Beth Moses
8. vii. 34

Dear Father Freud,

If one delays too long with a letter that one very much wants to write by hand, in the end one has to resort to the typewriter after all, in order to get rid of all that presses to be said. What presses here is not so much the enclosed letter, which I return to you with warmest thanks, but a medley of news and exclamations, which must go off to you. What a deep satisfaction there is in the events in Germany,[1] of which we have only had radio news so far. It transcends all our hopes that the real lords of Germany should have so quickly killed off their rivals. I gave the regime four years and now after 16 months one frightful gang of them has already been eradicated. It would be absurd to pretend that we are not delighted with what has happened, but I must say that the method employed and the people who carried out the purge

[1] Reference to the Röhm purge, June 30, 1934.

are such villains that they awaken a certain pity for the victims. And as long as Göring and Goebbels and Herr Hitler himself can still carry on unscathed, little is changed at the basis of the whole system and evil and infamy remain unvanquished in the world.

My second piece of news is that in order to have peace of mind to surmount the difficulties in my novel, in one fortnight I have written a play à l'improviste. It is called *Bonaparte in Jaffa*[1] and it's about Napoleon and the three thousand Turkish prisoners whom he captured in Jaffa and whom he had butchered. I am now going to let it lie for a little and as soon as the 'Habimah',[2] for whom it was written in the first place, have read it, I will send it to you. I think it might well be put on in Vienna, and if that were the case, this winter I could come over and stay for some time and be near you. For the moment, however, it is lying in my drawer here, waiting for certain small adjustments to be made.

And my last piece of news is that the Nietzsche plan is very gradually taking shape. I really need some action round which I can build a plot, which would make the whole thing independent of time and give it an epic sequence, and for this I am taking Nietzsche's central struggle to gain his independence from his family. You will agree with me that he was always in flight from his family, without ever being able simply to disavow them, and that the conflict from which he takes refuge in psychosis was obviously a family one. In order to bring out most forcibly the tragic quality of his ultimate defeat, we must show that at the conscious level this conflict involves his struggle against his sister's lust for power, as expressed, if possible, in matters of money, inheritance or similar concrete and trivial squabbles. The terrible thing in Nietzsche's fate is not the psychosis in itself, but the fact that the psychosis enables his sister to gain control of his entire person and of his work. Once I have this skeleton of

---

[1] A. Zweig: *Bonaparte in Jaffa*. Aufbau Bühnen Vertrieb, Berlin, 1949.
[2] Habimah: Hebrew theatre.

the book clearly before me, everything else will come of its own accord. Now, you have an intimate knowledge of the letters and of the contributions which we owe to Frau Förster[1] on this subject, and my eyes would have to do a lot of work, especially in the later volumes. But perhaps you could give me some tips to enable me to make some short-cuts and perhaps you could suggest certain epochs and episodes to which I should direct my attention. Naturally I shall no longer venture to approach Frau Lou, though I would gladly have details from her of a quite external nature: voice, clothes, accent, etc. Whether for example he spoke in Saxon dialect, his outward bearing, what impression he made, when he got rid of his bushy moustache, etc. But of course I can make all that up. The central point in my plan is actually the possibility it offers of discharging an anti-German affect more fiercely and totally than would be conceivable in any other way. Nietzsche's notorious contempt for German anti-semitism makes him absolutely vital as the hero of this novel. But before I get down to dictating it, much water will have flowed down the Danube or the Kishon.

For the time being I am struggling with my analysis, with a resistance which has increased and seems to provide us with a guarantee for a thoroughgoing investigation; and I am also struggling with the plot for my novel, which in the last few days has finally taken shape and sent forth shoots as it has not done for six years. If the material which has recently kept me awake at night bears fruit in the bright daylight hours of sunshine, I shall soon be able to plunge back into an extensive recall of the past and come to Europe in a few months with a hefty ms.

But do not imagine, dear Father Freud, that apart from you and Feuchtwanger[2] I have much to attract me over

---

[1] Elisabeth Förster-Nietzsche (1846–1935): Nietzsche's sister and administrator of the Nietzsche archive in Weimar, known to have tampered with Nietzsche's writings and letters.

[2] Lion Feuchtwanger (1884–1958): German author.

there. For today our children return, our flat is beautiful and we are very pleased with it. When your son Martin,[1] whom we are much looking forward to seeing, comes here he will be able to tell you all about it.

All good wishes from our family to yours.

Yours
Zweig

Vienna XIX, Strassergasse 47
15. vii. 34

Dear Meister Arnold,

So you have tossed off a new play at top speed, an episode from the life of that magnificent rascal Napoleon, who remained fixated on his puberty phantasies, was blessed with incredible good luck, inhibited by no ties apart from his family, and made his way through life like a sleepwalker, until he was finally shipwrecked by his folie de grandeur. There scarcely ever was a genius so totally lacking in distinction, an absolutely classic Anti-Gentleman,[2] but he was cut on the grand scale.

Curious as to how things are with you. You very much overestimate my knowledge of Nietzsche. And for that reason I cannot tell you anything that might be useful for you. For me there are two sentinels which bar the approach to the Nietzsche problem. First, it is impossible to understand anyone without knowing his sexual constitution, and Nietzsche's is a complete enigma. There is even a story that he was a passive homosexual and that he contracted syphilis in a male brothel in Italy. Whether this is true or not—quien sabe? Secondly, he had a serious illness and after a long period of warning symptoms he suffered a general paralysis. Everyone has conflicts. With a general paralysis the conflicts recede into the background of the aetiology. Should writers be

[1] Martin Freud (1889–1967): Freud's eldest son.
[2] In English in original text.

allowed to weave such a web of fantasy round the crude pathological facts? I do not know. Writers are not usually very amenable creatures.

Events in Germany remind me, by way of contrast, of an experience I had in the summer of 1920. It was the first congress outside our prison bars, held in The Hague. It is still pleasant to remember how kind our Dutch colleagues were to us starving, shabby Central Europeans. At the end of the congress they gave us a dinner of really Dutch proportions, for which we were not allowed to pay, but we had also forgotten how to eat. When the hors-d'œuvres were handed round, we all enjoyed them, but after that we were done; we could not take any more. And now to my contrast; after the news of June 30th I had just one feeling–what, I'm supposed to leave the table after the hors-d'œuvres! There's nothing more to come? I'm still hungry.

My son's chief assistant in the Verlag has been struck down with polio and so Martin will not be able to make the trip to Palestine. But when you come to Vienna, even if you are laden with the ms. of a novel, you will be welcome to

Your
Freud

P.S. Greetings to the ladies.

Carmel, Beth Moses
12. viii. 34

Dear Father Freud,

I do not know how long I have had your wonderful Napoleon-Nietzsche letter. But really I am in constant contact with you; every analytic hour sees to that; only what benefit is that to us both, to you and to me? I was too stupid and shy to ask you to look over my analytic state and the disturbing symptoms of my relapse were not properly visible till we reached Palestine. But if I had stayed in Vienna! I wish this only on account of you, for otherwise as an expelled alien one is well advised to get right away from German-speaking territory, i.e. to come here where one sheds one's Jewish national prejudices just as a dog shakes off his fleas in the water. But there are still enough positive features–human qualities developed in many different milieus–to make life here seem good to us. At any rate I can work, and where in Europe could I do that now? Unfortunately the theatre people have not returned my ms. of *Napoleon in Jaffa*–we have written to them three times about it – just think, my sole ms. in the hands of the theatre people, who are childish, narcissistic, unserious and unreliable! Tomorrow I am going to send a friend to Tel Aviv to get it from them. Then I shall get some typescripts made and you shall have a copy. Then you will see what my Bonaparte is like; a man of 29, ambitious, opportunistic, as yet not wi'hout certain standards of decency but unscrupulous–and on the grand scale.

I hope you can read this spidery writing. My good fountain pen was stolen from my desk, as before that was Dita's camera from her cupboard, while we were moving into the flat; and later, three weeks ago, Lily's beautiful new typewriter, which was my wedding gift to her, was stolen through the window of my ground-floor study. But as we are spending far more than we are earning, I am making do for the time being with the pen I use for correcting proofs. It's just that my writing gets too thin and shaky; it expresses less what I am than what I at the moment possess. What I am is diligent, fundamentally uncertain, productive, progressing well in my analysis, in the process of change.

You remember that you compared the Hitler murders with the hors-d'œuvres at the Dutch congress, by way of contrast. Well, in the meantime a particularly horrible dessert has been served up in your country.[1] What a generation we live in! Has not Senigallia long been outdone?[2]

<hr>

[1] The assassination of Chancellor Dollfuss, August 1934.

[2] In 1502, Cesare Borgia decoyed unsuspecting condottieri into his house in Senigallia and had them murdered.

Could we ever have imagined this? You do not need to revise your judgement of human nature, but the rest of us have to rethink our views constantly. These then are the Germans and Austrians—the people of the Alps and the Silesians, the Berliners and the Rhinelanders. And this is what the war forced out of them and what it has left of them. (This pen, borrowed, is no good either.) All my writing must be put on a new footing and that is what I am aiming at now in the novel which has been lying around, half planned, for so many years. What will be the outcome? 'Erziehung vor Verdun' is the theme of the book, and fortunately it permits me to peel off one skin after another, until I finally have the essential thing in my hands.

Meanwhile Nietzsche must slowly go on simmering. Every word you say on this topic is worth its weight in gold to me. I do not want to explain him, except through early anecdotes with his parents and his sister. Then I will shape the whole thing myself, in all its obscurity. As far as I can see at present, he had just one highly intensified characteristic—that was his fear of being devoured by his family, specially by Lisbeth. And that is precisely what does happen—to a monstrous degree, so that all that remains of him is the hollowed-out shell. Mother and sister devour him, as does the Germany of Bismarck and the Nazis, everything he despises. And his basic ideas are all carried ad absurdum: the loud Wagnerian element of his hero-cult, the Zarathustra-Liszt music, anti-socialism, everything. But there remains his personality, the wonderfully pure essence of his being, his courtesy of heart, his gentleness of manner, his quiet radiance, the halcyon Nietzsche, not a Dionysus but a human being, a sensitive nostalgic seeker after the vanished Ariadne, an island world of the heart and mind, which occasionally glimmers through even when he is completely benighted. This must all be put in juxtaposition to the rhapsodic isolation of Zarathustra; this will remain the permanent Nietzsche music, a Brahms quartet as compared with the Tristan din of *Zarathustra*.

And above and around him: Lisbeth with her bun and her assiduity, the spider who has eaten her mate and is now the mate herself. Oh, I would need many lives to give body and shape to all that teems within me! What should I read in order to study your theory of psychosis, apart from Dr. Schreber whom I already know?[1] Where in particular can I find something on paralysis itself?

Dear Father Freud, I am not worried about you because I think things have more or less settled down in your country now. But you are careful, aren't you? Give my kind regards to all your family, especially to Frau Anna. She will be hearing from Dr. Eitingon[2] how much need there is here for your art and hers. And please let me see your writing again soon.

Yours
Zweig

My family and Lily all send kindest greetings.

Haifa, Carmel
23. ix. 34

Dear Father Freud,

The twelfth volume is here! Hallelujah! Now I can read *Das Unbehagen*.[3] I had the Dostoevsky essay[4] read to me right away and was annoyed at the praise you pay to Stefan Zweig, who now sees himself as the impartial judge between the parties. But I have something much more important to tell you, something even pleasanter than my gratitude for your wonderful gift.

What I have to tell you is that my analysis is going well and that a miracle has taken place—my amnesia has been over-

[1] S. Freud: 'Psycho-Analytic Notes on an Autobiographical Account of a Case of Paranoia (Dementia Paranoides)'. *St. Ed.* XII, pp. 9 ff.

[2] Max Eitingon, Berlin psychoanalyst, emigrated later to Jerusalem.

[3] S. Freud: *Civilization and its Discontents. St. Ed.* XXI, pp. 64 ff.

[4] S. Freud: 'Dostoievsky and Parricide'. *St. Ed.* XXI, pp. 175 ff.

come. Something never remembered has been remembered, namely in a dream. According to a dream sentence my tonsils had been removed. I knew nothing of this. On waking at about 6:30 a.m. I gave the matter a great deal of thought and I recalled that in 1908 a doctor in the Munich throat clinic had insisted that my tonsils must have been cut, as I had only the roots left. At that time I had maintained that this was impossible, as I had absolutely no memory of it. I then fell asleep again and dreamt about a blonde woman, whose name escaped me, and also about a little girl whose name I could not quite remember either. Then in the analysis I remembered first that our doctor's name was Reichmann. Then I got the name of the blonde woman. She was called Frau Bogatzky and the little girl was a friend of our Michi and the sister of a small boy called Richard. And what did Dr. S. have to say to all this? 'Bogaty' in Russian means 'a rich man', and the form Bogatzky would correspond fairly exactly, in a somewhat Polish form, to the name Reichmann. Richard is also the English for 'reich mann'! You know, don't you, that I learnt some Russian for two years at school.

Is not that splendid, Father of Analysis? I think I understand why you have not yet replied to my last letter. But my contact with you has remained excellent and Dr. S. is good at his job. I see the results in my work and you will notice it in my novel.

Meanwhile I am sending you *Bonaparte in Jaffa* for you to get a proper reminder from me. I have rewritten Act V; it was conceived and dictated just ten days ago. Now the play is ready, though I have to put in a few little nails here and there. Do you know anyone who would recommend it to a good theatre in Vienna? Or is there no such thing in Vienna any more? I would like to earn some money with it and see it produced when I come to visit you after finishing my novel. Provided there isn't a war on. Heavens, what a state mankind is in! It is good to think that you grew up in an age when one could remain a whole man and develop in all directions. Is your health all right?

All the best wishes for you at home, among your books, at your work and in your collections.

As ever
Yours
Zweig

For not much longer Vienna XIX, Strassergasse 47
30. 9. 34

Dear Meister Arnold,

I am answering immediately as I am worried lest your Bonaparte play may have gone astray on the journey. But it may still turn up. You think you understand why I have not written to you for so long, but in fact you do not. Perhaps you suspect—and not quite without reason—that I did not want to disturb you any more with my continued objections to your Nietzsche project. But the real reason was different. For being somewhat at a loss what to do in a period of comparative leisure I have written something myself[1] and this, contrary to my original intention, took up so much of my time that everything else was neglected. Now, do not start rejoicing, for I wager that you will never get it to read. But let me explain what has happened.

The starting point of my work is familiar to you—it was the same as that of your *Bilanz*. Faced with the new persecutions, one asks oneself again how the Jews have come to be what they are and why they have attracted this undying hatred. I soon discovered the formula: Moses created the Jews. So I gave my work the title: *The Man Moses, a historical novel* (with more justification than your Nietzsche novel). The material fits into three sections. The first part is like an interesting novel; the second is laborious and boring; the

[1] S. Freud: *Moses an Egyptian?* Later enlarged to *Moses and Monotheism. St. Ed.* XXIII, pp. 7 ff.

91

third is full of content and makes exacting reading. The whole enterprise broke down on this third section, for it involved a theory of religion–certainly nothing new for me after *Totem and Taboo*, but something new and fundamental for the uninitiated. It is the thought of these uninitiated readers that makes me hold over the finished work. For we live here in an atmosphere of Catholic orthodoxy. They say that the politics of our country are determined by one Pater Schmidt, who lives in St. Gabriel near Mödling. He is a confidant of the Pope, and unfortunately he himself is an ethnologist and a student of comparative religion, whose books make no secret of his abhorrence of analysis and especially of my totem theory. My good friend Edoardo Weiss[1] has founded a psychoanalytical group in Rome and published several numbers of a *Rivista Italiana di Psicoanalisis*. Suddenly this publication was prohibited and although Weiss had direct access to Mussolini and had received a promise of help from him, the ban could not be lifted. It is said to have come direct from the Vatican and Pater Schmidt to have been responsible for it. Now, any publication of mine will be sure to attract a certain amount of attention, which will not escape the notice of this inimical priest. Thus we might be risking a ban on psychoanalysis in Vienna and the suspension of all our publications here. If this danger involved me alone, I would be but little concerned, but to deprive all our members in Vienna of their livelihood is too great a responsibility.

And in addition there is the fact that this work does not seem to me sufficiently substantiated, nor does it altogether please me. It is therefore not the occasion for a martyrdom. Enough of this for the moment.

Of my so-called health I prefer not to say much. At least it permits me to carry on my normal professional work. When these glorious autumn days are over we shall be returning to the Berggasse.

[1] Edoardo Weiss: Italian psychoanalyst.

92

The morsel from your analysis is very savoury; I hope I shall not be confined to such samples.

When your play arrives I shall pass on to Martin your question about getting it produced. We have not got many contacts with the theatre world. Your personal presence here will then be more or less essential. Certainly things do not look too good at the moment, but if under the influence of your remarks I think back to the time when I grew up, I cannot say that I am really sorry that that epoch is over. It's all much of a muchness, as they say.

Till I hear from you again, I shall be pleased to assume that you and your family are all well.

Ever yours
Freud

Carmel
11. x. 34

Dear Father Freud,

The contents of your letter this time have at once delighted and depressed me. The fact that you have again put on paper some of the findings of your unique understanding is of such inestimable importance to all of us that you must not keep them to yourself. On the other hand you are of course right in every word you say about the avoidable risk to psycho-analysis. So I would suggest that you have the work printed privately in a limited, numbered edition, which would not even be publicly announced. Through the Society you are assured of a definite number of subscribers to cover the cost of publication, and if you liked, you could have the ms. printed here and then you would be relieved of all anxiety. There would be an added spice in the fact that the place of publication would be Jerusalem. And then we would get the typescript here very quickly and would have the great honour and joy of being your first readers. So what do you say? Dear Father Freud, after the samples you give of the

93

structure and content of the book, there is probably nothing ready for print anywhere today so eagerly awaited as your 'historical novel'.

I am only now sending off the *Bonaparte*. I had to let it lie a little, as I needed to wait for 'after thoughts'. I look forward to your criticism; your judgement is simply vital to me, as public criticism just does not exist any more and it would take the sum total of public opinion to outweigh your decision, were I unable to accept it. When you condemned *Laubheu* so clearly and precisely, you did me a service, for you dissuaded me from wasting any more time on a matter which was neither fish, flesh, nor good red herring.

Barthou's[1] assassination has made things in the immediate future very uncertain. It is frightful: violence begets violence and stupidity stupidity. I was quite shattered yesterday. Clearly the Yugoslavs have a troubled history behind them to feel compelled to perpetuate it like this. Though Hitler is the only one to benefit, it will be hard to prove that he had a hand in this. But if there were the slightest hint that this were the case, it might give rise to a new torrent of events which would put an end to the Hitler epoch. But shall we have this joy?

I hope you continue to have a glorious autumn (such as we are having) and I send my greetings to all your family, especially to your Anna, on whose help I count in my plan for getting your book printed.

Ever yours
Zweig

Analytical details next time.

Vienna
14. x. 34

Returning to the Berggasse. *Bonaparte in Jaffa* not arrived.

Ever yours
Freud

[1] Jean Louis Barthou (1862–1934): French politician, murdered together with King Alexander of Yugoslavia by a Croat terrorist.

Bonaparte arrived; will be easy to read; shall give the manuscript to others to read. Thanks for your suggestions about the 'historical novel'. It would not do.

Ever yours
Freud

Haifa, Mount Carmel, Beth Moses
29. x. 34

Dear Father Freud,

I was delighted with your two cards, as I am indeed with every token of your hand; but I hope you will read Bonaparte yourself and that you will enjoy it. Practical matters should and shall be dealt with as of secondary importance: there is an agency with the pungent name of Pfeffer and there are other possible contacts too, e.g. Erich Ziegel's Viennese Kammerspiele–all this need not worry us. But what does worry me is the thought that you regard the situation as so menacing for psychoanalysis. Eitingon, to whom I passed on your comments in confidence, thought the danger to be less great and he maintained that if *Totem and Taboo* and the *Future of an Illusion* had not brought Pater Schmidt down upon you, then the Moses novel would not do it either. But a book that appeared long ago is one thing, a totally new one quite another. The latter might bring the trouble to a head; there I must reluctantly agree with you. But is this trouble inevitable? Could you not send a Moses ms. here? From what Eitingon says it must be a daring and exciting work; and from hints that you yourself have let fall, I get furious at the thought that we are to suffer such deprivation and that you should think of shutting up such a piece of work in a drawer, as Grillparzer did with his *Libussa*.[1]

---

[1] Franz Grillparzer (1791–1872): Austrian playwright. *Libussa* did not appear till 1873.

Tomorrow I am off to Tel Aviv, where Dita has a little exhibition of her work, and when I get back I hope the infernal resistance that is confronting Dr. S. and me at the moment will be overcome.

Then you will hear more from

Your
A. Z.

Vienna XIX, Berggasse 19
6. xi. 34

Dear Meister Arnold,

Pfeffers have just rung up about your ms. Naturally I read it with much enjoyment. As a character study it gave me great pleasure. I cannot judge whether it would be effective on the stage.

I have one criticism which I will not conceal from you: it seems to me too cruel, unjustifiably so inasmuch as it singles out a situation which manifests the horror and inhumanity of war itself rather than the guilt of any one individual. In one of Caesar's battles in Gaul it happened that the besieged (was it Alesia)[1] and Vercingetorix[2] had nothing more to eat. They then drove out their wretched women and children into the no-man's-land between the fortress and the besieging Roman army, and there the poor creatures starved miserably to death between their own people who could not give them anything to eat and the enemy who would not, or who perhaps had not much to eat either. It would have been more merciful to have killed them in the town. Faced with such decisions one recoils in horror without taking sides. It's like shipwrecked mariners deciding to slaughter one of their own comrades.

By the way, have I ever given you the analytic explanation of the phantastic expedition to Egypt? I do not want to repeat

[1] Alesia: Capital of Mandubia in Gaul; captured by Caesar in 52 B.C.
[2] Vercingetorix, Gallic general, surrendered to the victor and was beheaded in Rome in 46 B.C.

myself. Napoleon had a tremendous Joseph-complex. That was the name of his elder brother and he had to marry a woman called Josephine. His overwhelming jealousy of his elder brother had been transformed into warm love under the influence of his father identification, and the obsession was then transferred to his wife. Incorrigible dreamer that he was, he had to play the rôle of Joseph in Egypt, and later on provided for his brothers in Europe, just as though he had been successful in his conquest of Egypt. And by the way, we owe the deciphering of the hieroglyphics to this piece of folly on Napoleon's part.

I have written to Eitingon that you are right in your view that it would be a risk to get my *Moses* published. But the risk, though real enough, is not the only obstacle. More important is the fact that this historical novel won't stand up to my own criticism. I need more certainty and I should not like to endanger the final formula of the whole book, which I regard as valuable, by founding it on a base of clay. So let us leave it aside.

With warmest greetings and best wishes for the overcoming of your resistances,

Yours
Freud

Vienna XIX, Berggasse 19
16. xii. 34

Dear Meister Arnold,

Whew! what a plethora of plans and projects—it sounds almost manic. Is it your analysis that's liberating all this in you? Can it all be carried out? And what about my concern that your war novel will appear too late and will miss the interest which is already being claimed by the next war? By the way, I recently saw *Die Erziehung vor Verdun* announced in a bookseller's catalogue. If it had already appeared, I would have received a copy, wouldn't I?

Your description of how conditions in the Holy Land reinforce resistance to analysis is very impressive.[1] But you are not dismayed. There is more to be experienced than in the Kaffir village (*Negerdorf*) of Berlin.

Don't say any more about the Moses book. The fact that this, probably my last creative effort, should have come to grief depresses me enough as it is. Not that I can shake him off. The man and what I wanted to make of him pursue me everywhere. But it would not do; the external dangers and inner misgivings allow of no other solution. I think my memory of recent events is no longer reliable. The fact that I wrote at length to you in an earlier letter about Moses being an Egyptian is not the essential point, though it is the starting point. Nor is it any inner uncertainty on my part, for that is as good as settled, but the fact that I was obliged to construct so imposing a statue upon feet of clay, so that any fool could topple it.

I am having a bad time as far as my health is concerned. I am getting radium treatment in the mouth and I react to this diabolical stuff with the most frightful pain. One often thinks—le jeu ne vaut pas la chandelle.[2] One feels ill. Resolutions help little in face of the immediate, unambiguous sensation.

This letter will probably arrive in time to bring you and your family my best wishes for Christmas.

Ever yours
Freud

Haifa, Carmel
25. xii. 34

Dearest Father Freud,

I have been thinking about you constantly for several days. I dreamt about you too. I knew that I would be

[1] Arnold Zweig had given a detailed description in his last letter of all the transport difficulties involved in his visits to Dr. S. which made these visits both tiring and time-consuming.
[2] 'The game is not worth the candle.'

writing by the next airmail, so that my New Year wishes would reach you in good time. And now today your letter of December 16th has arrived. You are ill again. I have far too great a respect for your personal achievement in this battle with your illness to be able to talk about it. But what you have endured and still endure is done for us, and the simple act of breathing, so dearly won, is one more thing you add to all the other deeds of succour and revelation you have achieved during your life. So when the radium in your mouth tortures you, the image of your suffering tortures us in our imagination, and we press your hand in ever deeper gratitude. If the year 1935 is better for you than the end of 1934, if your indefatigable creative genius should speak again and find some other theme for its expression than Moses, whom we will always go on waiting for, then–and even without all this–we rejoice to know that you are still there with us and we greet you in gratitude and joy.

Now as to your question about the *Erziehung*: the book is, of course, far from being in print and the booksellers are counting their chickens before they are hatched. Just now I am engaged in working through it for the last time. As soon as it has taken on physical shape, you shall get a copy before anyone else, you know that. I have let it grow far too large and I must shorten and cut a great deal in the beginning and middle. On the other hand, thanks to my analysis, the last sections, the last third, are really successful and I can imagine you reading them now without blushing. A compositor called Pahl, an Eberhard Kroysing, lieutenant in the pioneer corps, and a Nurse Kläre send you their regards, not to mention W. Bertin and a host of common or garden creatures.

But if the plans I lay before you seem manic, I can't help it. Big plans and little plans keep on coming to me. Little ones, like *Bonaparte* or the enclosed poem, get carried out; big ones are carried round with me for a long time, or are postponed, and impossible ones are reabsorbed.

27. xii. Now it is raining again and there are great flashes of lightning, while yesterday was a day such as we do not get in the best of springs—everything sparkling with fresh green and the sky clear and blue like a dream. We are already picking narcissus and cyclamen on the southern slopes. Spring and autumn crocus flower together in November or early December. In Deganya on Lake Kinnereth the roses are already in full bloom—I saw a bunch of them yesterday at Dr. S.'s. He works well and consistently and helps me very much. I notice it in my work and from my children. They have both been somewhat tense; they withdraw from outer contacts, the older one into his books and the younger into dreams, and they love the family circle more than is good. But recently they have been showing an inclination to roam about again, which they had while they were in their homes, before our flat was ready.

And now a few words about the Lord Jesus. The enclosed poem is just a joke from an age gone by, when you could still write such things in German. If you would like to keep it, please do. For a certain period of time mankind seems to need this symbol of the sacrificial son. The masses would have had less understanding for the sacrificial ox of Serapis and for the mysteries of Mithras, and would have remained even more barbarian. There is no kind of reality in the Jesus figure and that is why, like the literature of puberty, it has been able to contribute to the formation of the super-ego, to absorb man's longing for self-sacrifice and to sublimate masochism. And with that I will say goodbye to you and yours for the last time in this year of misfortune, 1934, and remain in good times and in bad

Your faithful
Arnold Zweig

P.S. You have given me the title of doctor once again on the envelope. I accept it gladly at your hands!

Haifa, Mt. Carmel, House Dr. Moses
5. ii. 35

Dear Father Freud,

If I had not already heard in Jerusalem at the beginning of January that you were all right and that the torture with the radium had therefore been of some benefit to you, I would have written long ago to enquire about you. I wrote to you for New Year and enclosed a poem called *Die Schöpfungsromanze*, of which I had only the one copy. Did this little opus ever reach you? I myself have had my shoulder to the wheel the whole time, trying to shorten my novel, which had grown too long, and also to work through it and polish it up—as far as my eyes will permit. My left eye has for the moment taken umbrage on account of overwork and my right has still not come back from its vacation. But the resistance has now been circumscribed.

Ever yours
Zweig

Vienna 19, Berggasse 19
13. 2. 1935

Dear Meister Arnold,

Quite right, I *did* receive both your letter and the *Schöpfungsgedicht* and I have not replied. Why not? Your letter gave me great pleasure. Perhaps that's the very reason. Your description of spring made me sad and envious. I still have so much capacity for enjoyment that I am dissatisfied with the resignation that is forced upon me. It is a bitter winter here in Vienna and I have not been out for months. I also find it hard to adapt myself to the rôle of the hero suffering for mankind, which you kindly assign me. My mood is bad, little pleases me, my self-criticism has grown much more acute. I would diagnose it as senile depression in anyone else. I see a cloud of disaster passing over the world, even over my own little world. I must remind myself of the one bright spot, and that is that my daughter Anna is making such excellent analytic discoveries just now and–they all tell me–is delivering masterly lectures on them. An admonition therefore not to believe that the world will end with my death.

I will not bestow the title of Dr. on you any more; but give it instead to your landlord.[1]

Nothing can be done about *my* Moses. When you next come to Vienna, I shall be pleased for you to read the manuscript which has been laid aside so that you may confirm my judgement.

I shall send back your *Schöpfungsgedicht* since you have just the one copy. It seems to me to pay too much respect to the barbarous god of volcanoes and wildernesses whom I grew to dislike very much in the course of my studies in Moses and who was quite alien to my Jewish consciousness. In my text I maintain that the hero Moses had never heard the name Yahweh, that the Jewish people never were on Sinai-Horeb and that they never passed through the Red Sea, etc.

Surprisingly enough Dr. Ludwig Bauer, about whom I complained to you, has died. Not that his death affected me. It was not just that he abused his rôle as journalist but also the base way in which he defended what he had done. It was a painful disillusionment, yet another.

Farewell, write and tell your news to

Your faithful
Freud

And take great care of both your eyes.

Haifa, Mt. Carmel
1 March 35

Dear Father Freud,

My left eye is now suffering from overstrain, my right is not yet functioning, so I am writing without being able to see very well and the result is in keeping. But the thought

[1] Arnold Zweig lived in the house of the Zionist Dr. Siegfried Moses.

that I might be able to say something to you about your Moses and thus about the cause of your gloom is too strong and my feeling of gratitude to you too pressing to resist. Please read Elias Auerbach's[1] *Desert and Promised Land.* You will there find in print all the daring statements you touched on in your last letter. Horeb-Sinai etc. He treats only the historical factors but that he does thoroughly and the book is based on a critical and systematic knowledge of the Bible and its sources. There is just one step Au. does not take: he does not turn Moscheh into Mizri. It makes extremely stimulating, exciting reading and it is written with exemplary objectivity. So far I have just read the first 100 pages but you would find them of great interest. I am very pleased to be able to draw your attention to this work. Nothing mythological, just an attempt to write history.

On Tuesday I am off to Jerusalem. Perhaps while I am there Eitingon will be able to tell me something about your daughter Anna's discoveries and lectures. I would so like to know something of them and reading is out of the question. My work goes gaily on. Lily replaces my eyes by hers, by her patience, her assiduity and her sympathetic understanding. Dita has got stage fever. She is giving an exhibition of landscapes in Jerusalem on Tuesday: Eichkamp, Mondsee, Sanary, Carmel—very fine things. But I have my worries: it is difficult to balance our budget: my son Michi has outgrown his strength, has got something on his pleura, is too thin, is full of complexes. But all this can be endured. Could you not manage to take a trip here? Greetings to all, specially to the ladies

From your
Zweig

[1] Elias Auerbach: *Wüste und gelobtes Land.* 2 vols. Kurt Wolff Verlag, 1932–36.

Dear Meister Arnold,

Full of impatience I sent right away for Auerbach's history and I was disappointed in my expectations and confirmed in my opinion. My revolutionary new ideas are not dreamt of by A.; neither Moses' Egyptian nationality nor the derivation of his religion from Egyptian monotheism nor the fusion of his person with that of a Midianite priest who took up the religion of Yahweh in Kadesh about 100–150 years after him; nor the view that the miraculous delivery from the bulrushes and the passage into Sinai are phantasies and that Moses had never known the name of Yahweh. In brief, his Moses is not my Moses; he has not broken with tradition nor exposed the pre-history which tradition has always suppressed.

So much for my disappointment. My opinion about the weakness of my historical construction was confirmed and it was this which rightly made me desist from publishing my work. The rest is really silence.

These are tense and unhappy times for our poor Austria, caught between Communism and Fascism. *If* I come to Haifa I will certainly bring *Moses* for you. At the moment we are concerned about a more immediate object—our move to Grinzing. We probably shall not be able to get our nice house there again.

My wife is well, my sister-in-law is in Merano, my daughter and nurse busy.

You write very legibly, even without your eyes, to which I extend my best wishes.

Ever yours
Freud

Dear Meister Arnold,

On further reading I see that Auerbach also rejects the scene on Mt. Sinai. But the substitution of Sinai by Kadesh is not peculiar to me but is a conclusion of Ed. Meyer[1] and Grossmann.[2]

Ever yours
Freud

The misunderstanding of Egyptian pre-history in Israel's religious development is just as great in Auerbach as in the Biblical tradition. Even their famous historical and literary sense can only be an Egyptian legacy.

Carmel
30 April 1935

Dear Father Freud,

Once again we have reached the point in the year when we remember the day of your birth and according to tradition congratulate you on it. I would like to give you all kinds of things: good weather, joy in your garden, and the feeling of having achieved much and of having rescued the name of Freud from the oblivion into which we shall all pass, some sooner, some later, but you never – if the word has any meaning. And now I must already say goodbye to you, for my eye compels me to be brief; but on the evening of the 6th I shall raise a glass of wine in a toast to the great star of Venus which is now in the ascendant in the Western sky, and I shall drink to you and yours.

Ever yours
Arnold Zweig

My wife and my whole family join me in my gratitude.

[1] Eduard Meyer (1855–1930): Professor in Halle, Breslau, Berlin.
[2] Christian Gottlob Leberecht Grossmann (1783–1857): Professor of Theology in Leipzig.

Dear Meister Arnold,

I am sitting in my room in Grinzing, in front of me the glorious garden with its fresh green and reddish brown leaves (copper beech) and I note that the snowstorm with which May came in has stopped (or paused) and that a cold sun dominates the climate. My idea of enjoying spring on Mt. Carmel with you was, of course, only a fantasy. Even supported by my faithful Anna-Antigone I could not undertake any journey; on the contrary, I have recently had to undergo a cauterisation in the oral cavity.

I cannot say that much is happening in my world. Since I have not been able to smoke freely, I no longer wish to write, or perhaps I only use this as a pretext to veil the unproductiveness of old age. *Moses* will not let go of my imagination. I picture myself reading it aloud to you when you come to Vienna, despite my defective speech. In an account of Tel el Amarna, which has not yet been fully excavated, I noticed a comment on a certain Prince Thothmes, of whom nothing further is known. If I were a millionaire, I would finance the continuation of these excavations. This Thothmes could be my Moses and I would be able to boast that I had guessed right.

At the instigation of the Fischer Verlag I have written a short address[1] for Thomas Mann's sixtieth birthday (6 June) and I have slipped in an admonition which I hope will not pass unnoticed. The times are dark, fortunately it is not my task to put them right.

With warmest greetings

Yours
Freud

[1] S. Freud: 'To Thomas Mann on his 6oth Birthday'. *St. Ed.* XXII, pp. 255 ff.

Dear Meister Arnold,

A letter to or from Palestine takes so long that I am reply-
ing to you on the day I receive it. I write to you with
pleasure and with special ease and I notice that I write
many things to you which I would withhold from others.
In addition I have a lot of free time: i.e. very few hours of
analysis. People seem to have learnt that I am fairly old and
they no longer flock to me; accordingly I am slowly declining
but there ought to be a process of self-regulation between the
cause and the effect.

As to your questions:[1] no, I have not received any proofs
from you and I do not know which ones I should be expecting.
My son Oliver lives in Nice, where he has taken over the
direction of a photographic business. In this way he has at
any rate found work which satisfies his practical urges.

As far as my own productivity goes, it is like what happens
in analysis. If a particular subject has been suppressed,
nothing takes its place and the field of vision remains empty.
So do I now remain fixated on the *Moses*, which has been
laid aside and on which I can do no more. When may I read
it to you?

If your analysis has not been able to disperse the infantile
amnesia, it has certainly not shown its full power. This is not
the fault of the analyst. It often happens, especially in the
case of people of a practical turn of mind in whom no severe
sufferings or inhibitions maintain a strong conflict.

A proper analysis is a slow process. In some cases I myself
have only been able to uncover the core of the problem after
many years, not, it is true, of continuous analysis, and I was
not able to say where I had gone wrong in my technique.
It is the exact opposite of a mountebank like O. Rank[2] who

---

[1] Questions in an unpublished letter.

[2] Otto Rank: Psychoanalyst in Vienna and later in U.S.A. At first a
devoted follower of Freud, later went his own way.

travels around maintaining that he can cure a severe obsessional neurosis in four months! But partial and superficial analyses, such as you are having, are also fruitful and beneficial. The main impression one gets is of the marvellous quality of the life of the psyche. But it is a scientific undertaking rather than an easy therapeutic operation.

An unexpected honour came my way recently. I was unanimously elected an honorary member of the Royal Society of Medicine. This will make a good impression in the world at large. In Vienna dark goings-on are afoot, directed in the first place against the practice of child-analysis. At Whitsun we received a visit from our brave Italian colleague, Edoardo Weiss, from Rome. Mussolini is putting great difficulties in the way of psychoanalytic literature. Analysis can flourish no better under Fascism than under Bolshevism and National Socialism. God has much to put right there.

Do not be long in writing again. I can read your writing quite well.

Ever yours
Freud

Carmel
1 Sept. 35

My dear Father Freud,

It is nothing but great tiredness after my work is done that has kept me from sending you more of my ever more illegible handwriting. It is sad not to have heard anything from you but I try to put a good interpretation on it. One of these days now my novel will be reaching you. I have reminded Amsterdam innumerable times. And then I will hear what your impression is.

Meanwhile I have been going through various crises. Firstly, I have established quite calmly that I do not belong here. After twenty years of Zionism this is naturally hard to believe. It is not that I personally am disappointed, for we are really doing quite well here. But all our reasons for coming here were mistaken. And this became abundantly clear to me when a fortnight ago I joined in a big anti-war demonstration along with left-wing workers. They tried to keep up the nationalistic fiction that they did not understand me when I spoke German and so they had my speech translated into Iwrith—as though all 2500 of them did not speak Yiddish at home. And all this took place with the left-wing Poale Zion,[1] who are attacked by the other 'righter' Social Democrats as being international. So we are slowly thinking of leaving but it will all take some time.

Meanwhile I am working fast and furious at my plans for the sequel to *Grischa* which was announced eight years ago under the title *Einsetzung eines Königs*.[2] It will make a marvellous story, but I must do a lot more thinking before I get down to work. But the Nazis surely will not be in office any more when the book appears and if war can be avoided down here. I have explained to a friend in Geneva that Italy ought to be given half of German East Africa as a mandate. Will he hand the message on?

Ever yours
Zweig

Vienna
9. 9. 1935
Thanks for your letter. *Erziehung vor Verdun* just arrived. Congratulations.

Ever yours
Freud

[1] Poale Zion, Jewish Socialist Labour Party.
[2] English translation: *The Crowning of a King*. Secker and Warburg, 1938.

Dear Meister Arnold,

Master indeed! My daughter Anna is now reading the *Erziehung vor Verdun* and she keeps coming in to me and telling me her impressions. We then exchange views. You know that I imagine it was my warning which restrained you from returning to Berlin, and I am still proud of this achievement, and now it is more certain than ever that you should never go near the German frontier again. You are too good for that.

It is like a long-hoped-for liberation. At last the truth, the grim ultimate truth, which is nevertheless essential. You cannot understand the Germany of today if you know nothing of Verdun and what it stands for. It is true that disillusionment has come late in the day, even in your case. Hence the obvious anachronism that the education at Verdun is followed by the Grischa idyll where there is still little suggestion that all illusions are dead. This fits in with the fact that when the war was over you settled in Berlin and built a little house there. Today one says to oneself: If I had drawn the right conclusions from Verdun, then I should have known that I could not live among these people. We all thought it was the war and not the people, but other nations went through the war as well and nevertheless behaved differently. We did not want to believe it at the time, but it was true what the others said about the Boches.

The factor which completes the education of the hero is not as clear as in *Grischa*—that is perhaps a weakness in the book. But in the characterisation of the numerous figures you show your frankly incredible mastery. To set someone like Lieutenant Kroysink before us—how do you do it? By what means do you conjure a Schwester Klara into life? How did you manage to give what is after all such a charming delineation of the bird-faced Crown Prince? It would be interesting to question you one day about the 'day residues' which have gone into this composition. But Vienna must not have become German before you visit me.

With kindest greetings and with the expression of my most eager admiration

Your old friend
Freud

Carmel
22. 11. 35

Dear Father Freud,

On days like today I wish you were here: we go for walks and bring back the flowers we have picked on the way – autumn crocuses, crocuses, narcissi – and which are all now standing nicely on our mantelpiece. Nature everywhere makes up for the disappointments which mankind never tires of creating. But perhaps you, too, are having lovely weather and are able to go out a little to Hochroterd, where there must surely also be autumn crocuses. At any rate, the news I got of you from Dr. Eitingon when I lunched with him in Jerusalem was gratifying – in what good fettle you were, how much pleasure you were getting from your collections and how your enjoyment of the *Erziehung* was unabated. That is splendid, and you will be pleased to hear that up to a few weeks ago 3000 copies had already been sold. That's a large number by today's standards, for our readers have grown poorer and the press sees to it that large sections of Germans outside Germany never get to the point of enjoying our books. Foreign editions are being prepared in America, England and France and in Italy too – censorship permitting – and in Czechoslovakia, Poland and Denmark, but not here, nor in Sweden, where the book has already been turned down by three publishers and where the Nazis have a lot of influence. The Spanish edition will no doubt appear in the Argentine and there will be some delay before the Russian one comes out. Looked at this way, the world seems small, for the reading public everywhere is more or less the same. And there is no one writing today who could express an authoritative judgement in the name of all educated people or even for many of them, as Voltaire, Goethe, Lessing and Ruskin once did.

If only you would devote a few months to the writing of reviews of novels—I am not speaking professionally though I mean it professionally as well. In the German-speaking world nowadays, there is no longer any sense of values and standards; someone will have to re-create them. You have the authority: you have now and then commented on works of art and what you have said remains and serves as a stand-ard to all who know your works. And in matters of literary appreciation a whole school is indebted to you for its exist-ence. You like reading and you read a great deal. Have you started on Feuchtwanger's[1] *Söhne*? He continues the Jewish war in the same mature excellent style. An outstanding book. And what do you think of Henry IV?[2]

If you like I will send you *Bonaparte in Jaffa* in its final form. I have done a lot to the last two acts, and I still have a few details to add. I shall soon be plunging into the *Einsetzung eines Königs*. The vast amount of material cries out to be shaped and narrowed down, and it is this latter problem that preoccupies me. Am I not really obliged to sacrifice form this time and become German, i.e. formless, but should I not at least outline the breadth and depth of my theme, even if I know I shall hardly be able to master it in its entirety?

I have got ready for publication a small volume of essays of a descriptive character, a first collection of short secondary works. A second volume shall follow, if this first finds a publisher, with essays devoted to intellectual figures and their works. If the two short essays dealing with you should

[1] Lion Feuchtwanger: *Die Söhne*. Amsterdam, 1935.
[2] Heinrich Mann: *Die Jugend des Königs Henri Quatre*. Amsterdam, 1935.

not be among the works which have been rescued, I shall ask your son Martin to send me copies of them or of the volumes where they appeared. I would never have dreamt of making such a collection without including a really definitive account of your influence. But times have changed so much for the worse that one now has to be satisfied with provisional statements. One thing, however, I shall certainly do: in a few days' time I shall go into Jerusalem again and armed with pencil and paper I shall discuss with Eitingon what changes your work has effected or will effect in the most varied disciplines. I can add an essay like that to my first one on 'Freud und der Mensch',[1] if my memory does not mislead me. And something about your way of writing. You are *the* one living writer whose every sentence, without haste and without pause, communicates knowledge. Whoever reads your sentences one after another is forced to think as he goes along. And whoever misses out just one or two of these sentences is compelled to go back and begin again, or he will not understand anything further. This is a severe test for the 'intellectuals'. These people have accepted a certain standard – but it's a waste of ink to write about that!

I have now been here for almost two years and I can see that for Dita and the children and for my work I made the right choice, but as far as my own personal influence is concerned, both cultural and political, it is nil. People here demand their Hebrew, and I cannot give it to them. I am a German writer and a German European, and this fact has certain consequences. But where can I live if not here? Can a man like me come to Vienna, where every political utterance of the State would be repugnant to me, just as mine would be to the State? And where else is there to go? It is more or less the same wherever one is if one is not at home. . . .

How long do you think Germany will remain Brown? I am not expecting a red or even a pink regime to follow – though

[1] A. Zweig: 'Sigmund Freud und der Mensch'. *Die Psycho-analytische Bewegung*, 1929, Heft I.

that would be a logical development – but a liberally coloured monarchy, a grandchild of Wilhelm's perhaps, which would inspire confidence and acquire credits once it had got rid of the Brown regime with the help of the army. Perhaps no State can make sudden transitions and perhaps Germany has to catch up on the gap left by Friedrich III. This would be the most likely follow-on to the corrupters of the people, the leaders of the blind and the counterfeiters, as I call Herr Streicher.[1] All this is of course based on the assumption that we succeed in avoiding war and in preventing the Brown Pest from spreading. War would change everything, and just as the last war brought the partition of Poland to an end, the next one would undo the Seven Years' War and restore Silesia once again to Austria.

Are you laughing at my phantasies? But what else can I do? I cannot read, I have got no one now to read aloud to me, I think over moral decisions and political events and go through the happenings of the war all over again, and I set myself my old problem: either violence will prevail or the moral order. And I believe in the latter, probably with your agreement. However that may be I am

Always yours
Zweig

Haifa – Har-Harcarmel
Beth Dr. Moses
End of Dec. 1935

Dear Father Freud,

Your grandson[2] has just paid us a short visit and this afternoon he is going to tell us in greater detail all that he can concerning you, Vienna, himself, his plans and his hopes. I am not writing this letter by hand as I usually do, but on the typewriter, as I want to give you without delay certain

[1] Julius Streicher (1885–1946): Editor of *Der Stürmer*, an anti-semitic newspaper; executed at Nuremberg.
[2] The son of Freud's daughter Sophie.

114

news which I must convey with every precaution and care. To proceed chronologically: a journalist I have known for a long time and who worked even before the Hitler period for German newspapers in Egypt read to me some time ago passages of a report about Arab events concerning Ibn Saud.[1] He knows Arabic well, studied it in Berlin, continued his studies in Cairo and for a time lived in Luxor until the coming of Hitler deprived him of his employment and shipped him over here. Now, a few weeks ago he admitted to me that he had long been working on a play about Moses and he asked me to allow him to read it to me. This he did the day before yesterday, and this led to his giving me a number of pieces of information concerning his sources. His Moses is a pupil of the Sun Temple of Re-Aton and is a younger contemporary of Amenophis III. Extremely astonished about this dating of his, I asked him how he came to make this unhistoric chronology, secretly thinking, of course, of your great work and rather excited on your account. He maintained that a Professor Smith of the Rockefeller Museum in Luxor had told him that among the Tel el Amarna letters which were recently excavated, there was a small tablet containing a list of the pupils at the Re-Aton temple in Heliopolis and that among these were two names which could only be interpreted as being those of Moses and Aaron. He went on to say that this small tablet had been in the possession of a rich Coptic Christian, a landowner, who had then bequeathed it to the Vatican, where it is now kept. I questioned the man as carefully as I could, and I explained to him that one of my closest friends would be most interested to learn more about the matter. I went so far as to say that the publication of an extremely important book would depend on whether the scientific accuracy of this point could be established. Dr. Jizchaki (that is the name he now goes by) maintained that Professor Smith had given him the information just as he had now transmitted it to me.

[1] Ibn Saud: Founder of the Kingdom of Saudi Arabia.

You will see for yourself the weak spots in this account. If the man wanted to win my interest in his play by maintaining that he had sources for his interpretation, he could not have done better than to cite his sojourn in Egypt and those excavations, which I could not check on, and consequently I could not accuse him of having acted irresponsibly. On the other hand, I had never spoken to him about Moses, and he could have had no idea that I was in any way interested in the sources of his literary creations. He must have known that he did not make his play any better by propping up his imagination on archaeological crutches. Of course, the play is bad but that need not concern us here; all we need do is to ask ourselves whether it would have been possible for a man of so little creative talent to have invented this little clay tablet.

You possess the large Brockhaus, dear Father Freud, and you can look up and see whether there is a Rockefeller Institute or Museum. I am indebted to our friend Eitingon for the priceless gift of three volumes (supplement to the last pre-war edition) of the Encyclopaedia Britannica and so far I have found nothing in it on Luxor. But it happens that I know the assistant archaeologist in the Rockefeller Institute in Jerusalem and for a year she has been doing nothing except arranging the pieces of pottery there. She will certainly be able to tell me whether there is a Professor Smith in Luxor and whether excavated material can be purloined in this way. Judging by my experiences in Palestine one third of all excavated material is stolen by the natives and then sold privately, which they have every right to do. Otherwise I, for example, would not possess the double shekel of Strato II of Phoenicia which was struck in Sidon round about 400 B.C. nor a small coin from Ascalon, both of them with the trireme on the reverse side. I must have told you that I took back a little collection of coins from Palestine which Lily managed to rescue.

I cannot give you any further news today. But in a few

days I should hear from Jerusalem as to the possibility or impossibility of the existence of Dr. Jizchaki's tablet, and I will let you know the outcome right away. Meantime from the bottom of my heart I wish you a Happy New Year.

Yours
Zweig

Vienna, 27. xii. 35

Dear Meister A.,

I am not answering your letter yet, but I just want to say that I am eagerly waiting for further news. I found nothing about a Rockefeller Foundation in Brockhaus. The reference to Aaron makes the account given by your authority very dubious. I do not believe he, Aaron, ever existed. And the names cannot have appeared on the tablet in the traditional form.

Kindest greetings and auf Wiedersehen.

Yours
Freud

Haifa, December 1935

Information.

The application of the name Rockefeller Museum to the Institute in Luxor is more or less correct, since Rockefeller is a generous patron, but this is not its proper title. The 'Oriental Institute of the University of Chicago' has its headquarters in Luxor, which is the centre for excavation and research.

An enquiry in Luxor would be the best means of ascertaining whether a Professor Smith works there.

I regard it as impossible that tablets belonging to the Tel el Amarna finds should contain lists of the pupils of the Re-Aton Temple since these finds, which date back to the 1880's, consisted solely of letters and these are in general from foreign princes and consist exclusively of lists of gifts from these princes. I cannot at the moment ascertain whether other clay tablets were found in Tel el Amarna but this is certainly a possibility.

In Knudtzon's detailed publication of the tablets (1908) the Vatican is not cited as the depository of any of the Amarna tablets, but at that time some were in private ownership. But the answer to this question is of no significance at this juncture, since this publication can have no connection with the Amarna finds. It is not in itself impossible that some Egyptian clay tablets should have made their way to the Vatican, for stolen finds which have passed through many hands are frequently involved.

Dear Father Freud,

This is more than we had both expected. My scepticism quadrupled with each day that passed after I had sent off my letter to you, and I was delighted and relieved when your card arrived and showed that you had no very high hopes. Our investigations are now proceeding; they are directed in the first instance to Dr. Polotzki, the Egyptologist in Jerusalem, since he is our nearest source of information. I had a talk with Dr. Eitingon the day before yesterday and I think he will be just as pleased as I am at the results so far. My correspondent also tells me that there was a Professor John Merlin Powis Smith in Luxor in 1932, and from earlier conversations I know that my authority actually was in Upper Egypt in 1932 when he was still in good circumstances and represented the *Berliner Tageblatt*. Our investigations are thus beginning to be interesting and promising as befits a matter of such importance. Dr. Eitingon has told me how you are and about the position of analysis in Europe. Next time I will write more fully: today a mountain of correspondence lies in front and on top of your

Warmly greeting
Zweig

Dear Meister Arnold,

Have just received your Information; pleased that you are devoting so much attention to the matter. So it seems that your 'poet's' statements have not been completely snatched out of thin air, but here and there really do have their feet on solid ground. Luxor exists, Rockefeller subsidies exist, and so even does Prof. Smith. But one point which occurred to me later and which invalidates all our expectations is the following: if such a list of the pupils of the Sun Temple of On (?) was found in Amarna, it could not possibly be in cuneiform on a clay tablet. It would have to be hieroglyphics on papyrus. Cuneiform was used only for correspondence with foreign countries. So there is little hope of rousing my Moses in this way from the sleep which is his destiny. One of my young friends here, a Dr. Ernst Kris,[1] a well-known art historian and official at the Museum, has also made certain investigations along channels accessible to him.

So much for Moses, which is one of the temptations that should entice you to Vienna. Another would be my promise to read you my last piece of work which most unfortunately must be published. I have been very much besought to write something for Romain Rolland's 70th birthday and have finally agreed. I managed to write a short analysis of a 'feeling of alienation' which overcame me on the Acropolis in Athens in 1904,[2] something very intimate with scarcely any connection with R. R. (apart from the fact that he is exactly the same age as my brother[3] with whom I was in Athens at that time). But combine the two proverbs about the rogue who gives more and the beautiful girl who will not give more than they have and you will see my situation.

[1] Ernst Kris (1900–56): At the time of Freud's letter an official at the Kunsthistorisches Museum, Vienna; later psychoanalyst in London and New York.

[2] S. Freud: 'A Disturbance of Memory on the Acropolis'. *St. Ed.* XXII, pp. 239 ff.   [3] Alexander Freud, 1866–1943.

As a result of a recent 'small' operation in my mouth I can now neither chew nor speak properly. I can but wait till it's better.

As ever
Yours
Freud

Berg Carmel, Haifa
15. 2. 36

Dear Father Freud,

That you have had to and been able to endure another operation fills me with regret and with joy. May this go on for a further ten years! May it now be granted us to offer you some further fruits of your life's work! My eldest son, Michi, is now in analysis with Dr. S. and is very satisfied. He was so terrified of his driving teacher, a Herr Schneider from Vienna who is harmless enough but who sometimes gets very angry, that Michi realised his fear was abnormal and decided of his own free will to have treatment. He is already considerably better. Not so, alas, his father. I am going through a bad crisis. I struggle against taking up my analysis with S. again, but also struggle against my whole existence here in Palestine. I feel I am in the wrong place. Restricted circumstances, restricted still further by the Hebraic nationalism of the Hebrews, who refuse to permit any other language to be used for publications. So I have to lead a life in translation. And if I am going to be translated into English, then why here? You have doubtless read poor Tucholsky's letter[1] and my reply. More about him some other time, perhaps in print. He died of his Jewish exile, literally. But what am I to do? Where could I settle with any prospect of permanence? My reason says 'In America'. But my heart does not want to go so far. It comforts me,

[1] Kurt Tucholsky (1890–1935): German writer. He committed suicide.

chameleonlike, with the hope that in a few years Germany will be accessible again and be able to make good use of me. What do you say? You and no one else restrained me from the folly of returning to Eichkamp in May 1933, i.e. to the concentration camp and death. Apart from you, of all my friends it was only Feuchtwanger who saw so clearly. But what do you advise me to do? I want to visit you this summer. If I finish my novel earlier, I will come in the spring. If I am finished by the end of April, then I will come in May. It would be sad to miss your 80th birthday. But before that I must make a bitter decision. My passport runs out in April. I do not want to ask the Third Reich for an extension. But I do not want to sever my connection with the German people of my own accord. I can get a Palestinian passport—in a few weeks. But I have also got little contact with Jewish nationality. I am a Jew—heavens, yes. But am I really of the same nationality as these people who have ignored me ever since *de Vriendt* came out? I want to fight only on one front, against the barbarians. I am perhaps too tired to strike out on all sides like an old donkey. At present the children too do not want to stay on here, though they speak Hebrew well. But they are learning almost nothing, wretched schools, narrow horizons. Ah well, I will end at that point for today. By the way, have you read Feuchtwanger's *Söhne?* An excellent book, most rewarding, written with clear, serene artistry. Perhaps there will soon appear in the *Weltbühne* a joke of mine, an autobiographical one called 'My Mishaps'.[1] Fare well, fare very very well. It is good to be able to take my bearings from you.

That is a solace to your

A. Zweig

[1] A. Zweig: 'Meine Unfälle'. *Die Neue Weltbühne*, Paris, 1939, No. 9.

Dear Meister Arnold,

Your letter moved me very much. It is not the first
time that I have heard of the difficulties the cultured
man finds in adapting himself to Palestine. History has never
given the Jewish people cause to develop their faculty
for creating a state or a society. And of course they take
with them all the shortcomings and vices in the culture
of the country they leave behind them into their new
abode. You feel ill at ease, but I did not know you found
isolation so hard to bear. Firmly based in your profession
as artist as you are, you ought to be able to be alone for a
while.

In Palestine at any rate you have your personal safety
and your human rights. And where would you think of
going? You would find America, I would say from all my
impressions, far more unbearable. Everywhere else you would
be a scarcely tolerated alien. In America too you would have
to shed your own language, not an article of clothing but
your own skin. I really think that for the moment you should
remain where you are. The prospect of having access to
Germany again in a few years really does exist. Sometimes I
even anticipate seeing this happen myself, and I am not
hoping for an extension of my life but for a curtailment of
the Nazi regime. It is true even that after the Nazis Germany
will not be what it was, not Eichkamp any more, so to
speak. But one will be able to participate in the clearing-up
process.

It will be a great joy to have you with me in Vienna-
Grinzing. We will forget all misery and criticism and indulge
in our phantasies about Moses. It does not need to be just
near my birthday; any other time is perhaps better. I do not
yet know how I am going to escape the exertions they will
expect of me but I certainly do not intend to join in. And what
nonsense to try to make up for all the ill-use of a lifetime by

celebrating such a questionable date! No, let us rather remain enemies.

Hoping to hear from you very soon

Ever yours
Freud

A young Berliner, a dentist from my daughter's family, will soon be visiting you.

Haifa, Mt. Carmel, House Dr. Moses
2. iii. 36

Dear Father Freud,

I am sorry that it is with my typewriter that I have to express my gratitude and joy in your gift and I have to tell you, too, that so far I have not been able to enjoy these six beautiful coins to the full. Your messenger, that swiftly spoken Berliner, together with his brother, arrived on Saturday afternoon. But on Friday afternoon, owing to the combination of a sudden change in the weather together with an enchanting motor drive, I burst a small vein in my left eye. This is the eye with which I could at any rate decipher parts of a line of reading and which permitted me to write by hand. The new blood clot covers only a minute part of the area of vision, but it is just the most important part, and in addition it has weakened the whole eye to such an extent that for the time being I must use it as little as possible. I also have to rest a good deal—this is excellent for thought and reflection but not exactly conducive to gaiety. I know that compared with your sufferings and your fortitude all this is not worth the fuss that this letter appears to be making. And I am not making a fuss. But it does depress me that my state of health is not more robust and that all the care and rest I have bestowed on my eye have not managed to give it greater powers of resistance. This car trip was only a short one and I made it once before without the slightest ill-effect. We went on a very decent though not asphalted road into the most beautiful valley full of trees in blossom and of indescribably lovely flowering meadows. Was the car not heavy enough this time or had the change of weather that afternoon suddenly increased my own blood pressure? On the journey itself I noticed a slight pain and by the evening I recognised the familiar clouding of my vision. It is quite possible that the minute particle of liquid will be absorbed by the eye and that everything will be all right again in a few weeks. Then I shall be able to appreciate the enchanting engraving on the coins with my magnifying glass and have them classified by an expert. Dr. G. told me that two were from Crete and one from Cyprus. And gold coins, dear Father Freud, were just what were lacking in my collection.

To return to your letter, I would just like to mention today the question of my visit. Accidents apart, I will come this year as soon as I can get away. But if you wish to celebrate your birthday in seclusion I shall not mind so much if I am held up and arrive later. Fortunately May is a good way off and things have time to develop in two months. Oddly enough we keep getting conflicting reports from Vienna. But the good news about a reaction against the Nazis is unfortunately not incompatible with bad news about the attitude towards the Jews. It is maddening that for the moment I cannot think of going into Jerusalem again to see the Eitingons. Theirs is the most delightful ménage in Jerusalem, and it is wonderful to have people so close who are so intimate with you and who carry out your work so faithfully.

And now I wish you the same peaceful harmonious life which all your visitors report to me and with my little family I remain

Ever yours
Arnold Zweig

Dear Father Freud,

It seems right that I should begin my birthday letter today as I do not know in how many instalments I shall write it. Since you have had far more to do with doctors than I have, you will know better than I how much heed one should pay them. In my present state nothing appeals to me more than writing to you—nothing is more animating and delightful when I am alone—and at the moment my unsatisfactory modus vivendi brings a certain emptiness with it. My wife and children also want to have some life of their own; they are healthier and younger than I and so they cannot be expected to have regard for all my needs and I cannot take it amiss that I am alone for many hours of the day when I would prefer to be in company and vice versa. But I *do* miss my reading and nothing can replace that. Even being read aloud to is not the same. To be alone with another mind, for instance this dialogue with you, re-reading *Totem and Taboo* or turning up some other of your volumes—all that is irreplaceable. I have tried it but it just does not work. I must therefore make do by means of thinking and remembering or else by means of productive work. Today for example I have finished off the end of an essay that the *Neue Tagebuch* asked for on your life and achievements.[1]

I worked at it for three days, pleased and depressed at one and the same time, for I did not want to describe publicly my personal relationship with you and yet that was uppermost in my mind throughout, just as a recent experience is uppermost in one's hour of analysis. And I could not let the publishers down, and it takes quite a time for the post to reach Paris. I also felt how much I would like to have absorbed your complete works once again before embarking on this essay, which is intended for you to read. Now I have sent it

[1] A. Zweig: 'Apollon bewältigt Dionysos'. Paris, *Das Neue Tagebuch*, 1936. Heft 18.

off and I can only hope that the demon who controls misprints will be merciful and that you will be able to read the essay ten days before it is returned to me here. Reading between the lines, you will realise that through your very existence you have made my rebirth possible and that I am profoundly happy when I see that human life has been put right through your achievement, and in fact that the distortion of human life has become reparable through you. But people understand all this only when it is pointed out to them. That is why I toy constantly with the idea of writing your biography—if you would permit me. I am ill-equipped to do it as I cannot read now but I am well-equipped in that I have personal experience of your work and also because I love and revere you and because I know what a figure such as you, what a man such as you, signifies.

25 April. Now much time has passed and much blood has flowed. If one can judge from the results, certain Englishmen must have profited from the Arabs[1] being prevented from going to London and that's what many fools do conclude, though the masses obey other laws. But we will not touch on that today. It would seem that one of my typewritten letters to you has gone astray, sent off towards the end of February or the beginning of March. And now I will conclude for today. I would like to send you some things for the 6th, but will it be possible? At any rate you must know that I feel proud and grateful for your friendship which I regard as the one honour mankind has to bestow nowadays and which I accept with delight.

    With greetings and congratulations to your wife

Yours
Arnold Zweig

[1] Reference to disturbances which took place in Palestine during the British mandate.

Dear Meister Arnold,

'The world's tenderness is indeed mixed with cruelty.' For two weeks now I have been using up every odd half-hour with filling up cards of thanks, like the one enclosed, and adding a few words or sentences underneath my signature, stilted and forced for the most part, and only today, on the first day of the pleasant Whitsun holiday, can I settle down and write you a letter, alarmed by the threat that you want to become my biographer—you, who have so much better and more important things to do, you who can establish monarchs and who can survey the brutal folly of mankind from a lofty vantage point; no, I am far too fond of you to permit such a thing. Anyone who writes a biography is committed to lies, concealments, hypocrisy, flattery and even to hiding his own lack of understanding, for biographical truth does not exist, and if it did we could not use it.

Truth is unobtainable, mankind does not deserve it, and in any case is not our Prince Hamlet right when he asks who would escape whipping were he used after his desert?

Thomas Mann's visit, the address he presented me with, the public lecture he delivered in my honour were gratifying and impressive events. Even my Viennese colleagues honoured me, and betrayed by all manner of signs how much against the grain it went. The Minister of Education delivered polite, formal congratulations and then the Austrian newspapers were threatened with confiscation if they reported his tribute inside the country. Numerous articles in newspapers at home and abroad expressed their repudiation and hatred clearly enough. One could thus establish with satisfaction that honesty has not yet quite vanished from the earth.

For me the date naturally marks no epoch; I am the same as before. Among the not very numerous gifts of antiques I received, your very remarkable signet ring gave me pleasure.

And now with warmest regards I await further news from you.

Yours
Freud

Haifa, Mt. Carmel, House Dr. Moses
8. 6. 36

Dear Father Freud,

I hope the internal and external upheavals will be slowly settling down again now and allowing you to slip back gradually into your normal way of life, of which Dr. Eitingon gave me such good reports before he left for Vienna.

Unfortunately I have not had a talk with him since he got back, but from Dr. S. I have learnt the main thing, namely that you have come safely through it all. I myself had got ready a few manuscripts for you which I thought you might like: a short play about the prophet Jonah, a somewhat longer one about the farmhand Jockel, who was asked to go and cut the oats, and finally a little anthology of verse parodies, dating from 1914 with an introduction on how they came to be written. I could not give the manuscripts to any-one to bring you and my paralysed condition after my rest-cure made concentrated work impossible for me. And I also did not want to send them by post, because at the moment I have not much confidence in our postal system. When things are unsettled, manuscripts tend to rouse suspicion, and once this happens, they easily get lost. But since things do not seem to be getting any better here, rather the opposite, I am sending off the little anthology of poems as Noah sent off the dove, with the intention of continuing if the first one arrives safely. May it and the insight it affords give you pleasure.

Meantime I have not been idle in my investigations on behalf of Moses. A young historian of Judaism, who lives near us on Mt. Carmel, has promised to look up a series of references made by earlier writers who were of the opinion that Moses was an Egyptian. Would this help you? I have still had no news from our Egyptologist. Following this train of thought brings me to your anxie ty on account of our friend Pater Schmidt. Obviously nothing has happened in that connection after all.

When I suggested in my handwritten letter that I should write your biography, I did not know that you were rendering such a book superfluous by extending your own autobiography.[1] By so doing you make such an undertaking unnecessary for a considerable time ahead, specially if you were to write at some time an account of the most important breaks you have had with former friends and pupils, in order to clarify objectively what really happened. No doubt these secessions will one day play a large part in the history of psychoanalysis and hence in an important sector of contemporary life.

I am in a strange state. After a long interval I have started serious work once again on my novel and at the same time I have resumed serious work with Dr. S. So my journey has to be postponed; I do not yet know for how long. All I do know is that I have an urgent need to get right away from this difficult country for some time and to breathe in the air of other personalities through conversation with the few friends who still remain.

Today the Verlag sent me a number of prospectuses and from them I learn with pleasure about all the new work that is in progress. I see for instance that your Anna has tackled a theme which I will get a friend to read to me in Europe once my own analysis permits. Altogether the precepts of the therapy will be to blame if I go to my grave cured but an ignoramus.

With this sombre prognosis, uttered with a smile and the warmest greeting, I leave you.

Yours
Zweig

[1] S. Freud: *An Autobiographical Study* (1925). *St. Ed.* XX, pp. 7 ff.

You will see, dear Father Freud, that our thoughts have more or less crossed. Indeed, had my son Adam not forgotten to take this letter to post, it would have gone off yesterday, four hours before yours arrived. By the same post my friend Stutschewsky sent me a copy of the *Wiener Illustrierte* with a picture of you with Zofie's puppies at your feet. That was a happy coincidence for which I am grateful. We must always tell ourselves one thing: people of your calibre were always treated in the past more harshly by their contemporaries than has been your lot in the Periclean days of Francis Joseph and Kaiser Wilhelm. If only you keep well and remain as sardonically cheerful as ever.

Yours
Zweig

Vienna XIX, Strassergasse 47
17. 6. 1936

Dear Meister Arnold,

The posthumous poems of Herr Floriz Capschon (Capzen?) together with historical introduction and letter from A. Z. arrived safely yesterday. They prove him to be a talented if loose young man: the eternal problems of the male gave him ample material for his verses.

There is one passage in your letter which I do not like because it shows me how little I know about you. It is the bit about 'my paralysed condition after my rest-cure'. I am happier in the fact that you no longer want to write my biography. But you should not incite me to write another chapter of my life-story. A survey of all the secessions that have taken place might easily lead to indiscretions and unpleasantness.

I am well aware of my privileged position as a member of the modern world. And I count it to my credit that our arch enemy P. Schmidt has just been awarded the Austrian decoration of honour for Art and Science for his pious lies in the field of ethnology. Clearly this is meant to console him for the fact that providence has allowed me to achieve the age of 80. Fate has its own ways of making one altruistic. When my master Ernst Brücke[1] received the award, in the midst of my awe I became aware of my own incipient wish to be similarly honoured one day. Today I am content with having been indirectly responsible for another's achieving it.

My Jofie is a stickler for accuracy and does not like being called Zofie by you; Jo as in Jew.

I gladly accept your offer of a list of the writers who acknowledged Moses to be an Egyptian. But not one of them made anything of the fact.

Thomas Mann, who delivered his lecture on me in five or six different places, was kind enough to repeat it for me personally in my room here in Grinzing on Sunday 14th. This was a great joy for me and for all my family who were present.

I quite understand, though in principle I am sorry to hear it, that your journey to Europe should be postponed. My father and my brother Emanuel[2] only lived to be $81\frac{1}{2}$. My Anna is very good and efficient.

With kind greetings and with good wishes for your eyes

Yours
Freud

Vienna XIX, Strassergasse 47
22. 6. 36

Dear Meister Arnold,

Your ship sails a month from today. The post takes so long that I must answer at once. And I do not want to put off any longer writing to tell you how pleased I am that your eyes are better. The improvement is visible even to others.

[1] Ernst von Brücke (1819–92): Professor of Physiology in Vienna, Director of the Physiological Institute.

[2] Sigmund Freud's half-brother, Emanuel Freud (1836–1917).

You must bring Looney back with you. I must try him on others, for obviously with you I have had no success. Your Shakespeare theory seems to me to be as improbable as it is lacking in foundation.[1] The most personal of Sh. works, his sonnets, show an elderly man who regrets much that has happened in his life and who pours out his heart to a younger man he loves. This youth is an aristocrat, probably H. W. Earl of Southampton. Actually the poet reveals himself unambiguously at one point when he mentions that he once carried the baldachin (i.e. over the Queen's head in a procession). So I warn the poet A. Zw. against building fantasies about Sh. on untenable premises.

One of your promises you did not keep: there was nothing in your envelope about your correspondence with Emil Ludwig. From what I hear he, along with Masaryk, was the only person who refused to sign the address for my 80th birthday. Last summer I was the victim of a painter called Victor Kraus who is married to a cousin of E. L. He told me frightful things about his behaviour.

The climate of the times, and also the happenings within

[1] In a letter from Carmel dated 12 June, 1936, Zweig had written: 'We shall have a lot to talk about concerning Shakespeare. Certainly no one has shed so much light on Shakespeare's biography as this Mr. Looney. But by equating the man who had the experiences and the poet he puts it all in doubt once more. The author of the historical plays was the passionate friend, the effeminate lover of an aristocrat, not an aristocrat himself. He was in violent opposition to his father, to the middle classes and to the artisans. He destroys all women who might be his rivals in his relation to his father, involves them in parricide, or disguises them as boys. Much might be said about the poet's identification with the passive woman, in the case of both Shakespeare and Goethe. Your splendid Dostoevsky essay, your *Theme of the 3 Caskets*, your *Poet and Fantasy*, your *Leonardo*—all these need only to be applied to the problem of Shakespeare. But they really must be applied. Looney has no notion of all this. I'll tell you the bold plan I have re William Shakespeare. Cervantes was an aristocrat, and Montaigne too. Shakespeare worshipped the past, because the middle classes were already knocking at the door.'
Freud had been very impressed by Thomas Looney's *Shakespeare Identified in Edward de Vere, 17th Earl of Oxford* (London, 1921).

the International Psycho-Analytical Society, do not make us very cheerful. Austria seems bent on becoming National Socialist. Fate seems to be conspiring with that gang. With ever less regret do I wait for the curtain to fall for me.

We are in Grinzing for the fourth time and I must admit the garden has never been so beautiful.

Looking forward very much to seeing you.

Yours
Freud

Haifa, Mt. Carmel, House Dr. Moses
16. 7. 36

Dear Father Freud,

Today I just want to let you know that I shall have my passport in a few weeks' time and that I shall therefore be ringing your front-door bell in August. I hope that you are once again comfortably accommodated in the Hohe Warte or elsewhere and that you are in as good fettle as political developments permit. I unfortunately am politically involved even in my work and I always seem to be caught up in something. I am perturbed at the fact that in all the reconstruction going on here, basic principles are even more neglected than I at first realised, and I am distressed to see how little has been done to foster Jewish-Arab cooperation, the necessity for which should be obvious to any reasonable person. But subterranean or even preconscious and conscious power-dreams and ambitions have made it impossible to introduce what is indispensable: mutual concessions within the territory we occupy in common.

I have begun my analysis again: this time we are going deeply and laboriously into childhood history, and we are discovering surprising cave paintings and enigmatic inscriptions which we are slowly deciphering. But it is exhausting work and I am often depressed and I almost dread interrupting the analysis though I desperately need relaxation and a change of air. But the moment that work on my novel came to a halt at a particular and characteristic spot, i.e. where things begin to go badly for the hero and I felt no inclination to crack this difficult nut, I realised that the time for the final struggle had arrived. I am working at this new novel now, so that I can send the first instalments off to the printer, even if I have to put off the final parts till I return. I will bring the manuscript with me if you would like to read this half-finished product, the work certainly will not meet with a better, kinder or more experienced critic. It is characteristic, too, that at the moment this novel suffers from spinal curvature; at some places it makes extravagant zig-zag bends whereas it should be quite straight, if it is to support all the ribs that branch off from it.

But all that can be discussed much better by word of mouth. I only hope that I shall be breaking in on one of your good periods, end of August, if I am not mistaken. Take care of yourself meanwhile, dear Father Freud. I already look forward to arriving on your doorstep and to seeing how well you have survived the exertions of the month of May, and you will read me some of your *Moses*, won't you? I have got no news to report on this front; my little philologist has gone to London to visit his parents-in-law without leaving me the promised compendium on Moses as an Egyptian. But he will give it to me later on. Please excuse this type-written letter; warmest greetings from my family to yours and please send a kind thought to

Your
Arnold Zweig

P.S. I was very pleased to hear of Thomas Mann's kind gesture. Altogether he now makes a very lively impression from a human point of view. But what do you think of his Joseph novel? What is your opinion of it as a whole and in parts, as to subject-matter, style and form?

Dear Father Freud,

When Dr. Eitingon came to visit us, it was not settled when I should be coming to Vienna—whether the middle or the end of August. Now it is decided that I shall sail on August 7th as Hermann Struck and his wife are also going to Vienna then and I could scarcely expect to find better travelling companions. Until my doctors have given their verdict, I am bound to regard a railway journey as a risk I do not want to run if I know I have no one with me who could help were I to have a set-back. But now all our minds are at rest and though my little Adam had a bowel upset a few days ago and though these last ten days will be very full of work and preparations, I am delighted that I shall be seeing you and your family so much sooner than I expected. I intend to ring you up on the 14th: est hic surrexit.

Till then I send warmest greetings as harbingers of my coming.

Yours
Arnold Zweig

Carmel, 1 Feb. 37

Dear Father Freud,

We have just spent a week in Jerusalem with Eitingon, who was alone at home and wanted visitors to cheer up his loneliness. We heard from him that you have again had to have a small operation and that Jofi is dead. Since then I have not been able to get the memory of that beautiful, noble, intelligent creature out of my mind. We are silently agreed about the epoch we live in where terrible things are happening to mankind all over the globe and every moment, even now while I am writing this and you are reading it. But that does not take away from the weight of loss we feel when something we love dies, even though it is a creature clad in its natural coat and not in a bought one. Jofi was a foster-child, as devoted to you as any real child and with a wiser heart than most of our children. That she should have been taken from you before her time is a kind of barbarism on the part of fate, which since the war has been getting far too practised in such cruelties. I hope Jofi's daughter will make up to you for what you have lost in her mother. But it will never be quite the same.

I am tormenting and amusing myself with the Shakespeare. For the time being I have given up having the Oxford books read aloud to me, and I want first to learn the biographical data as compiled by the orthodox believers. At any rate it is certain that his meeting with Oxford was a decisive landmark for Shakespeare, more decisive than Goethe's entry into Schiller's orbit. But I am not yet convinced that this means that Oxford was the writer of the plays. A whole gamut of questions centres round the problem.

You will be pleased to hear that my myopia has now improved by $1\frac{1}{2}$ diopters. This is a matter of subjective and objective opinion of both patient and doctor. I am also in very good spirits; I drink my carrot juice, take my pills, smoke tobacco sparingly and drink a little glass of red wine every evening. But this shall all come to an end before long. It would be even better if I could say that I am now able to read for longer and even do some work once more. This latter would also be very important from a financial point of view. We manage not only to balance our budget but also to make up for past losses, but this has been achieved only through American miracles, the Book of the Month, for example. Without these exceptional bonuses we would only just get by, as both Dita and Michi have been or rather still are in analysis, and things like dentists' bills, my treatment, doctors' fees, high rents (14 I.P. per month) and wages are a great burden upon me. I cannot afford to take taxis into the country and so I will not see much of the country this spring. But Carmel will do instead and so will our (miserable) railway line, if I want to visit Jerusalem or the young city of Tel Aviv with its new port. I almost forgot to say that I gave a lecture on 'Emigration and Neurosis' which is worth having duplicated for you and which therefore shall be done once my novel is finished. And please accept this little photo with love from Dita and from

Your ever faithful and grateful

A. Z.

Carmel, 21. 3. 37

Dear Father Freud,

Why should we not meet this year since it is certain that we shall all be coming to Europe this summer, unless some terrible accidents intervene. There is just one difficulty—we shall have to come by the cheapest route and that will be to Marseilles, between £6–£9 return, fare to Paris inclusive. But I have already started to make enquiries in Prague about delivering a lecture there; perhaps I will give two there and one in Brünn. Then I shall be quite near Vienna and my visa is valid till well into October. So it may be late in the year, but I shall certainly visit you and your family. But it would be kind if you could prolong your stay on earth somewhat. You have granted us $81\frac{1}{2}$ years, but this will not benefit us if we finally turn our backs on Palestine. And that we shall do next spring. It is financially impossible to carry on here. I am too far away from all chance of earning money in between writing my two long novels. We need more than I can in normal circumstances earn these days, despite stringent economies and without running a car or having many servants in the house. And how much the Russians will be able to alter this position remains to be seen. They certainly promise to pay. But in the first place not one of my novels has appeared as yet in Russia and secondly I am sceptical about the chameleonlike character of their system of publishing.

To stimulate my imagination I am occupying myself with Shakespeare in my leisure hours. I am still no subscriber to the Oxford theory, and if it were not you who had drawn my attention to it I would have arrived at the following conclusion: the Oxford researches provide the best, indeed the only, contribution to a biography of Shakespeare we possess. Certainly Oxford had a profound influence on Sh., indeed regenerated him, as it were. I cannot go into detail here about what he meant altogether to Shakespeare. You know that better than I do. He is, however, not the author of Sh.'s works, but the begetter. Much more so than Herder was of the young Goethe's. The feminine element in the poet thus comes into its own. He is able to conceive, is made to vibrate and by way of the short cuts of the imagination he lives through the life of others. Even Shakespeare's aristocratic element is 'begot' in this way. It is not inborn but is implanted in him. Like that of poor Nietzsche, the son of a court tutor. I would be pleased to hear whether you agree with me on this. The middle-class intellectual set against the true aristocrat. Nietzsche compared with Tolstoy or even Kropotkin, that is Shakespeare vis-à-vis Montaigne or Cervantes. As de Vere died in 1604, there must be some trace of his death in Sh.'s work. Ah well, we must talk about all this. I would like to write Shakespeare's 'Autobiography' in the spirit of the weary despairing man who died in Stratford: of the dramatist who developed out of the theatre just as did Molière, Lessing, Iffland,[1] Richard Wagner, Wedekind[2] and Brecht. Perhaps you will be able to share my interest in all this, though it does not fit in with your attitude to the question. But I can only think as I do, and you more than anyone else have enlightened us as to the degrees that exist between influencing a work and actually creating it.

[1] August Wilhelm Iffland (1759–1814): German actor and dramatist.
[2] Frank Wedekind (1864–1918): German poet and playwright.

Do you notice that my eyes are doing well? I am already reading once again. Anna's *Ego*[1] and your *Pleasure Principle*.[2] Both works give me great pleasure, but yours is the man and the *Ego* is the woman. As is right and proper. The splendid clarity you both have in common. The suppleness of the *Ego* and the irresistible movement of the argument in the *Pleasure Principle* are both equally admirable and convincing and the boldness of your observation rejoices my heart. Dear Father Freud, all this you have ventured on our behalf and you have not done it in vain.

Eitingon spent a few days with us here on Mt. Carmel, and next week we intend going to Baalbek and Damascus together.

Greetings to all
Yours
Zweig

Vienna IX, Berggasse 19
2. 4. 1937

Dear Meister Arnold,

I quite understand that you should want to leave Palestine, not just because you are cut off from your source of income but also because of your isolation in the nationalistic atmosphere there. So I may count on seeing you at the end of the summer or in the autumn. My hereditary claim on life runs out, as you know, in November. I would like to be able to guarantee it up till then, but I really do not want to delay any longer than that, for everything around us grows ever darker and more ominous and the awareness of one's own

---

[1] Anna Freud: *Das Ich und die Abwehrmechanismen*. Vienna, Internationaler Psychoanalytischer Verlag, 1936; *The Ego and the Mechanisms of Defence*. London, The Hogarth Press, 1937.

[2] S. Freud: *Beyond the Pleasure Principle*. St. Ed. XVIII.

helplessness ever more pressing. And so I do not wish to be fobbed off with the thought of your making your visit to Europe any later. So do not postpone it. We will have a lot to discuss about Shakespeare. I do not know what still attracts you to the man of Stratford. He seems to have nothing at all to justify his claim, whereas Oxford has almost everything. It is quite inconceivable to me that Shakespeare should have got everything secondhand—Hamlet's neurosis, Lear's madness, Macbeth's defiance and the character of Lady Macbeth, Othello's jealousy, etc. It almost irritates me that you should support the notion.

I was very pleased that you thought so highly of Anna's work. She has grown into a capable, independent person who has been blessed with insight into matters that merely confuse others. To be sure, for her sake I would like—but she must learn to do without me, and the fear of losing vital parts of my still intact personality through old age is an accelerating factor in my wish.

Schönherr,[1] who received a decoration for Arts and Science on his 70th birthday—the one thing your correspondent would still like to achieve, since it was conferred upon his master Brücke—must really be a great poet, for in his public acknowledgement he invented the word 'Dauererkältung' [chronic catarrh] which I might also use to describe my condition of many weeks past. Even the oldest people here, I among them, cannot remember such wretched spring weather. We had meant to go to Grinzing in three weeks' time, but will we be able to?

A fragment of Moses has found its way into *Imago*, but I wrote and told you that, didn't I? I am growing forgetful. I have already seen your novel advertised, so it will soon be coming my way.

Warmest greetings
Yours
Freud

[1] Karl Schönherr (1873–1943): Austrian writer and dramatist.

Dear Father Freud,

Every day I have been meaning to write to you, every day I prefer to read or to have read to me some of your overwhelming, liberating works. There is so much I do not yet know at all, and in a way I have got new eyes and ears for what I have already read. I am still quite shattered by the Ratman[1] and the Wolfman,[2] as my own analysis lies somewhere in between these two. I had to give up analysis last May as Dita and my elder son, Michi, were in need of its help and apart from Dr. S. there is no one here in Haifa. Some time before this crisis, in an experience with a young woman I had such a relapse that I had to start right again from the beginning. S. now knows a great deal about my situation, but I wonder constantly whether I should not come to you yourself. I have made a survey of my condition which is a somewhat complicated one. But it is not yet finished and I am still considering improving the plan of this survey, perhaps making it of general use by defining one special case. I would like so much to express my gratitude to analysis in general and not only to you personally.

You have no idea with what *care* for your method of working I read your writings. You are a scientist of a calibre such as mankind has never produced before. What you deduce from a case, an impulse of the psyche, an inhibition, a dream or a symptom, always puts me in mind of Newton and the apple. I could arrange to be within easy distance of you next year, I mean for a considerable period. But the political situation makes it difficult as I could not publish anything in Vienna, or so it appears now. And then you talk of leaving us, and it is certainly true there never was so revolting a time as this. But what are we to do then? Shall we let you go without a

---

[1] S. Freud: 'Notes upon a Case of Obsessional Neurosis'. *St. Ed.* X, pp. 155 ff.

[2] S. Freud: 'From the History of an Infantile Neurosis'. *St. Ed.* XVIII, pp. 7 ff.

word or should we tell you that you must not yet leave us
here alone? Ah, dear Father Freud, we must leave it to
you to decide whether you continue to follow in your
father's footsteps or whether you now move over into your
mother's tracks, which would still give you more than a
decade.

Anyhow, I shall be visiting you in Grinzing in July, and
then . . .

Ever yours
Zweig

Carmel, 1 May 37

Dear Father Freud,

I now feel a certain hesitation at sending off the two
pleasantries I prepared for your birthday. You might well
cast aside the one about Goethe in irritation, and not even
smile at the 'cover memory'. But we had to arrange some
little display of fireworks for you, and it often happens at
such displays that the man being celebrated or the guest
of honour gets his sleeve a bit singed. I am saying all
this to salve my own conscience, for my intentions were
really of the best and it was meant in the most congratulatory way when at Eitingon's suggestion I wrote down a
joke that had been improvised by me for our meetings in
Jerusalem.

And now I wish you good weather and au revoir. Today
it is hot here and as dry as in the desert, doubtless with you
it is cold and miserable. But your birthday is an event here
with us and we celebrate it and you by reading your works
and realising with joy how much healthier, happier and more
productive we have become through your lonely struggles,
and this applies to our children too: I must tell you more
about Adam sometime.

Best wishes to all your family whose lives have been

spent and are still spent in such love and fidelity alongside you.

Full of gratitude and joy

Yours
Zweig

How many volumes are there in the Sophien-Ausgabe of Goethe's works, letters included?

Vienna XIX, Strassergasse 47
Whitsunday, 16. 5. 37

Dear Meister Arnold,

No, I was just amused by your two pleasantries, as far as I am now capable of being amused, for weeks of pain have ended by making me grumpy and this time I find the post-operational reaction is lasting particularly long. Your essay on Goethe seems somehow to parody the Shakespeare theories with which, it appears, I had little success with you, but it is only a remote echo. I cannot tell you from here, Strassergasse, how many volumes there are in the Sophien-Ausgabe. The Encyclopaedia Britannica, Brockhaus and my own collected works make up my entire library here.

It has at last become lovely in the garden. One cannot help thinking of the words in the 'Spring Song':

Die Welt wird schöner mit jedem Tag,
man weiss nicht, was noch werden mag.[1]

Then one is faced with the contradiction. One knows there cannot be much more.

With warmest greetings and auf Wiedersehen

Yours
Freud

[1] Quotation from 'Frühlingsglauben' by Ludwig Uhland. Translation:

'The world grows fairer with every day,
And what may yet happen, no one can say.'

Dear Father Freud,

There can be no question that anything of yours has ever met with lack of success with me. Firstly, you have completely destroyed my naïve pedagogic certainty in matters relating to W. Sh. Secondly, through your intervention you have made Oxford an important figure for me, an heir-apparent to the highest poetic rank. Does that count for nothing? And thirdly, since our last conversations in October you have tempted me to create a Shakespeare character of such a kind that in the last weeks of his life he struggles with the shade of Oxford and all the time wishes to confess: My plays are not by me at all, they're by him. But I cannot decide—as yet—whether this should be a genuine confession or whether it is just a delusion. I am simply not convinced that the works are not by W. Sh. of Str. Why should they not be? Because we have no proof that he ever went to school? Or because he made money and bought land? Dear Father Freud, what do we know about Shakespeare's contemporaries—Kyd, Peele, Greene, Webster and Massinger? Two generations of Civil War swept away all records. And the fact that Shakespeare tells us he carried the baldachin well? Dante tells us that he has been in hell. The poet's idea of truth is peculiar; it refers to the reality of his ideas, not to the content of experienced reality behind these ideas. But we will soon be talking of these and other things—how happy I am at the thought!

I was delighted to read a short essay in the last number of the *Neue Tagebuch* on your Moses article. But my memory of the whole work is so vivid and so precious a possession that I do not want to have my total impression clouded by being reminded once again of how much we are losing by your suppression of the book. We have discussed your reasons, they are good reasons; out of regard for your decision I have said nothing publicly about *Moses* and the reasons for its suppression, though I would like to have paid you a tribute of gratitude and respect in the newspapers here. But a discussion of Clerico-Fascist reactionary forces in Austria would inevitably have come out of this, and that could only have been annoying for you. But at any rate I am exceedingly pleased about this respectful, perceptive and obviously youthful writer and from now on he has in me a more attentive reader than heretofore. While this article was being read to me, I remembered a few other non-native leaders – inter alia Prince Eugene in Austria, Helmuth Moltke in Prussia and what about Lycurgus and Solon? I will tell you in person about all the smaller and larger upheavals that have occurred in our household recently – anyhow they have brought about a total rearrangement of my books and now on the top shelf of the bookcase stand your eleven volumes in splendour and stripped of their dust jackets alongside thirty volumes of Goethe and a small edition of Nietzsche on wood-pulp paper.

And now I will wish you good weather, such as we are enjoying, and happy hours every day in your garden with your nearest and dearest. And as we are not leaving till the 21st (with Eitingon once more) perhaps you will write to me again.

Sincerely, as ever
Yours in gratitude
Arnold Zweig

I will bring my novel with me for you.

Zurich
10 August 37

Dear Father Freud,

To explain our silence: while we were having a meal in the dining-car, Dita's trunk, together with all our things, was pinched from the train – whether by mistake or on purpose, it was gone. We stayed three days in Obernberg on the Brenner to give Innsbruck time to make enquiries. My frightful catarrh got so much better in the marvellous air there, that I could talk in an undertone without my throat getting sore. Meanwhile the trunk has not yet turned up; we are making further enquiries. We went on to Lucerne, somewhat rested, installed Adam in the Bergsonne, the children's hostel on the Rigi, bathed in the lake and yesterday came on to Zurich to buy some new things for Dita and to arrange our visas and tickets for the journey home. We are very tired and somewhat depressed. The time we spent in Vienna with you in the warmth of your whole household will come into its own full radiance again once we have come to rest somewhere and can think over the whole period and all that happened. We had no idea we were so in need of rest; it is frightfully hot everywhere, it's true.

I am writing by lamplight when I should not really do this. I am still very hoarse and have so far not got into touch with Basel where post is awaiting me.

With warm greetings and many thanks from us all to you all

Yours
Zweig

I will send you our address later.

Amsterdam, Mervedeplain 3
6 Sept. 37

Dear Father Freud,

You will believe me implicitly when I tell you that I think of you constantly, every day, not just when I am putting on or taking off your splendid ring. This time so much remained unsaid: my joy at finding you so well and your family so pleased was so great, and at being able to introduce my Adam to you on whom my heart hangs as Jacob's did on Joseph. And in the time since we left you, I have had to do so much writing in connection with the trunk, theatres,

146

publishers and contracts that my eyes have really been achieving miracles. About you, all I could do was think.

Now I am on the scent of a piece of comparative philology which proves the identity of Yahweh and Jove from a linguistic point of view, and a Professor Yahuda[1] has promised to let me have his works on Egyptian influences in the Old Testament. These are being got ready for you and shall be sent to you, though Yahuda's contribution will follow later.

The weather is glorious now and the Jewish New Year's holiday tempts me to go out to Zandvoort. But I have engaged a secretary here, Lily's sister by the way, and I am finishing the eighth part of my novel, so that you will soon have Winfried's first rebellion against Claus to read, 'son' versus 'father'. My American publisher's arguments convinced me right away. This Hungarian Jew, who is a native of the same town as S. Fischer, knows a great deal about form and the art of the novel and about the demands of the reader and business matters as well. Here I can dictate very nicely the material I have ready. The three-year-old daughter of my obliging Ruth guarantees my always having something charming close at hand, and when I meet Dita in London I shall have the pleasant feeling that my novel is *really* finished. Both in Basel and here various theatrical projects are afoot, which will make a longish trip to Europe next May almost essential and it will pay for itself!

That is all for today by way of a greeting and a call on you. My throat is still not entirely better and I cannot smoke – here of all places! I hope you are quite particularly well.

With warmest greetings in filial affection

Zweig

[1] A. S. Yahuda (1877–1951): Jewish theologian and philologist; nine months later Freud's neighbour in Elsworthy Road, London.

Dear Father Freud,

This is my first morning in Paris and the first moment I have had to collect my thoughts, and it too is not going to be of much use to me, since all kinds of annoying mail was waiting for me here and my trunk, sent off in advance a fortnight ago, has still not arrived at the hotel but is at the Customs. But I must get in touch with you right away and tell you that I paid a most enjoyable visit to your son Ernst in London. He is calm, cheerful and full of youthful energy, and his house is charming in its simple dignity and modernity. I am always sorry you do not travel any more. You should sample the comforts of modern travel and visit your children and grandchildren in London. It is a wonderful way of getting about if one has no heavy luggage.... I flew, namely, from Amsterdam to London.

The one maddening thing is that I shall probably not now be going home via Vienna. The stars continue to be inauspicious for this trip. In the *N.T.B.*[1] I found an item concerning *Grischa* in Yiddish and in my post there was a similar one about *Semael*. Up till now I have only been rooked by all the Yiddish lords of the theatre. Vienna did not bring me in a halfpenny, Poland so far only 200 Zloty, so I must now see to it that we are not robbed of comparatively large sums. Propaganda against our works is considerable; sales in England and from the German editions are mediocre, and for the next year my prospects so far are pretty dim. But I am defending myself vigorously. And that's just it; I shall perhaps have to be busy from now till the 27th, both here and in Basel, where my agent lives. But I will be back again in June and if it is at all possible, perhaps even in early May, and naturally I shall come and visit you. Don't be angry with me this time, dear Father Freud.

[1] *N.T.B.*: *Das Neue Tagebuch*; German émigré journal published in Paris.

Kind regards to Anna and to all your household, both from Dita and especially from your

A. Z.

My throat is still wretched.

Excelsior Savoia Palace
Trieste
27 Oct. 37

Dear Father Freud,

The last line on this trip shall be to you. I have just telephoned Eitingon and he told me that you were really extremely well. What more can I ask? Bathed in sweat, I sit at my desk and for a moment I look towards Vienna and you; then I look back at my paper again and give you a tender, grateful nod (I am always bathed in sweat these days. To judge by my glands everything is an exertion for me. My throat is still wretched—nose and trachea likewise. Ah well, I can cope with all that.) The Verlag, like all publishing firms, sent me the wrong thing, i.e. the number of *Imago* containing the first fragment of *Moses*. It should have been *Analysis Terminable and Interminable*.[1] Well, I am now looking forward to getting the right number.

And now: auf Wiedersehen till the spring. Many things have cropped up which I must get down to during the winter months. Then I hope they will come to fruition in Europe. Theatre, Bonaparte.

To you, to Anna and to all your household I wish health and prosperity. You will be reading something of mine in November—end of November. And then you shall tell me whether it was worth my altering my trip for it. I think it was.

Ever yours
Zweig

---

[1] S. Freud: 'Analysis Terminable and Interminable'. *St. Ed.* XXIII.

149

Dear Father Freud,

The year shall not go out without my telling you how I
have been getting on so far. Since I saw you my novel
Einsetzung has appeared and you will have received a copy
and you will be able to judge the effect of the last two
sections and see how they have turned out. These were the
two that cost me so much trouble when I was so exhausted
on my trip to Europe. They prove to me once again that the
realistic standards of someone with a knowledge of the
reading public really meet the demands of form better than
the writer himself is able to. The fact that the book is so
rounded out and complete is really due to the matter-of-fact
demands of the Americo-Hungarian Jew B. W. Hübsch.[1]
He told me that no reader could be expected to wait for two
years to find out in the next novel what happened to the
hero. But enough of this. A few days ago I received my first
copies and they made a good, satisfactory impression on me.
I have watched this novel maturing over ten years, without
seeing it suffer damage, despite all my inhibitions, and I
have put all my formative energy into the last two sections—
all under your treasured and cherished patronage. And now
I am having a break and being idle, going in to Tel Aviv to
see Lily, who has now joined her husband there. I am taking
pleasure in Dita and the children and in the wonderful
country round us, and I am looking after my eyes in a cool
but careful way.

Tel Aviv. 12. 12. 37

I am now dictating what I should have written by hand
yesterday. But too many visitors arrived and a batch of post
that had to be attended to right away.

The oculist I am consulting here is a young Viennese, a
Dr. Much. He was assistant in Kiel to Heine, who invented
contact lenses, and subsequently he was assistant in the

[1] Editor, The Viking Press, New York.

ophthalmic hospital in Lucerne. There he studied the effect of amyl nitrite on diseases of the back of the eye, and he supervised and treated eight such cases of which he later wrote up accounts. I took his publications on the subject to my very cautious G.P., Dr. Meyer-Brodnitz, and after a consultation with him I decided to try inhaling doses of amyl nitrite daily. You know, I am sure, that amyl nitrite causes an expansion of the arteries and accelerates the flow of blood; it thus enables the eye to reduce and indeed overcome any disturbing scotomata through the improvement in the alimentation of the retina. The cases Much treated showed an astonishing improvement in vision; in some cases, indeed, the eye was restored to complete normality. The majority of his patients were only a little younger than I. A few, indeed, were older and all were kept under supervision for a considerable period, ranging from six to eighteen months, and in not one single case was there any subsequent deterioration in the eye nor did the effect of the treatment wear off. The odd thing is that once again my medical intuition has been proved right; for six years I have been telling everyone that I did not need an oculist but a physiologist, who would be able to improve the alimentation of the area behind the eye without the increase in blood pressure causing the bursting of new blood vessels on the surface. If the Gerson treatment was a first successful step in this direction, it now seems to me that this use of amyl nitrite is a second step whose effect is more rapidly apparent. On the average the results could be observed after the first ten days and they then increased in potency right up to the end of the treatment (about thirty days in all) and, most valuable feature of all, the sight continued to improve after the cessation of the treatment.

Various thoughts have occurred to me while I have been considering these matters: what caused the insufficient alimentation of the retina in my case and why should my TB have attacked the back of my eye, if the TB theory is correct, which the doctors here certainly doubt. Both my father and my mother had abnormal vision; my brother suffered from a loosening of the retina and my sister had nine diopters in her spectacles. There was therefore a hereditary disposition to weakness of the eyes. In my case, neurotic factors must have played an additional part since from childhood I was unusually dependent on my eyes and therefore my contraction of the arteries, which was psychologically motivated, brought about this weakening specifically of my sight. I expect we will have a chance to discuss all this.

I have agreed to attend the meeting of the P.E.N. Club in Prague in June. As I am not embarking on any more large-scale work but have a lot to finish up, I hope this time I will be able to come to Europe in May and, circumstances permitting, I trust I shall have plenty of time for the beautiful countries east of Germany. It is indeed sad that Austria is not feasible as a country for me to settle in and for the children to be educated in. For the economic situation would be no different for me in Austria than it is here in Palestine. And however much we might prefer Vienna—in order to be near you—from a political point of view I should be rendered just as ineffectual and be far more endangered than I am here where they showed me much kindness on my 50th birthday. You will understand that this does not affect our decision to leave here, but Dita and I both have a horror of further emigration. Neither of us is young enough to adapt easily or even with moderate difficulty to new conditions of life unless these are compensated for by an immediate improvement in our financial position. And where would that be the case now? So I am working to finish my play *Bonaparte in Jaffa*, as the actor-director Gustav Hartung in Basel has a stage for it and is determined to put it on, together with other plays of mine, as soon as he gets the manuscript. But do you think any financial gain is to be expected from this in the German-speaking lands? The most I can hope for is that Prague and Brünn will take the play, and if a miracle occurs and the rivalry between Zurich and the up-and-coming

Basel is not too acute, perhaps Zurich will put it on too. But where else? Not even Vienna will put it on. But I must make the most of this opportunity, as there is a remote chance of the English and American theatres' showing an interest after the German première takes place. In England and America the agents, adapters, producers and directors claim in all 50 per cent of the takings. . . .

It is now one o'clock. I have just come in from the sea; it is warm, glorious sunshine. Swimming makes me happy. Altogether things are going very well for me just now and for all those around me. And I hear the same of you and am deeply grateful.

In the meantime I thank you for being what you are and I remain your happy and grateful

A. Z.

Dear Meister Arnold,

Fine, a letter with only good news, some of it indeed very good, such as the report on the improvement of your eyes. If that remains so or they go on improving I shall try to think more kindly of amyl nitrite. It was given me when I had my heart trouble, and I hated it because it gave me such unpleasant sensations of congestion in the head. And you have had your 50th birthday without my being able to send you my warm congratulations on a half-century of artistic creativity and struggle.

I would have answered earlier had I not been waiting for the new chapter of the *Einsetzung*. When the book arrived we sent it straight away to our friend Dorothy Burlingham, who had just gone into a sanatorium for treatment of a recurrence of TB. Anna returned from there with the news that the story is continued beyond Bärbel's death and that we must wait till the book comes back to us.

Doubtless your practical adviser was right when he said that one should not let readers wait two years for a story to be concluded. But I would have preferred a second volume. By shortening it in this way some aspects, for instance the political, have suffered. In your interest I can scarcely regret that you have not chosen Vienna as your new home. The Government here is different but the people in their worship of anti-semitism are entirely at one with their brothers in the Reich. The noose round our necks is being tightened all the time even if we are not actually being throttled. Palestine is still British Empire at any rate; that is not to be under-estimated.

I will be sending a copy of *Moses* to you before the year is up. It will certainly cause a stir in a world that is hungry for sensation. Several offers from America and even from England to publish a *Psychoanalysis of the Bible* with the appropriate firms. I recognise the fact that I am not famous, but I am 'notorious.'[1]

My catarrh remains the same; that at any rate is faithful.

With best wishes for next year

Yours

Freud

Carmel, Haifa
30. Jan. 38

Dear Father Freud,

What a lot there is to say and to ask today! First of all warmest thanks for your letter of Dec. 20th which really deserves a whole page to itself. But first I must ask something that has been worrying me for days. An article by André Germain, reprinted in the *Palestine Post*, hints that there is a possibility of your deciding to leave Vienna. The fact that some member of the gutter press has insulted you would not be sufficient to uproot you from there. But if you wanted to

---

[1] English in the original.

establish a freer, more humane and fairer atmosphere for the last years of your life and to publish *Moses* in your lifetime—what wonderful fruit to spring from the abominable soil of Austro-Nazism!—then we would never need to travel via Vienna again, or to board an Italian ship, or to gaze at the disgusting faces of the Viennese petit bourgeoisie—one could just sail from Haifa to Marseilles, or fly to London or take an orange boat to Liverpool or Southampton, and there would be a direct line between us. And if we should decide to leave this country we would try to be near you and to arrange things so that we could meet frequently. But this is all probably not true. You have had your bad experiences with the wild men of the newspaper world and you will stay on in Vienna and we will come to visit you during your lifetime and after. . . . Your achievement will in any case be sufficient to guarantee the immortality of Viennese cultural life in the 19th and 20th centuries. The second part of *Moses* alone would suffice to do that! It gave me such pleasure. Not just because it revived memories for me of the hours when you read aloud in your garden, and indoors, this work which, now in print, will move and stir intelligent people as it stirred and convinced me as I listened. A few objections will be made to it, e.g. you must certainly know that the transposition of names from one dominant culture to another was usual in antiquity and in the Middle Ages as it is today. But the whole argument in all its caution and intrepidity cannot be neglected any longer.

10. ii. 38

I am quite unable to say for what good or bad reasons the despatch or rather the continuation of this letter was delayed. You know it was certainly not indifference on my part. Rather the opposite. I had some correspondence with Dr. Eitingon, arising from André Germain's article, about your plans to move from Vienna. Then I dictated a long essay on the Ten Commandments which I mean to send you as I think you will enjoy it. There is a section in it on the First

Commandment which really has acquired meaning only through your *Moses*. For it affirms that it was Yahweh who delivered the Jews from Egypt. A very necessary step since in that way the peace between the Levites and the Yahwites of Kadesh was sealed. Then I finished my *Bonaparte in Jaffa* and am just waiting to get Act V before I send it to you. And finally I am preparing for publication a youthful novel of mine; it was written in 1909 and the story takes place in 1908. I wanted to tell you about this. But there are now such odd things in the papers that I am first of all hastening to enquire how you are and what plans you have for the next few weeks. It is so strange to think that you are not really obliged to live in Vienna and that you are spending your peaceful old age there of your own free will. Please give my warmest greetings to your wife and to Anna and to all your household.

Yours
Zweig

Carmel, House Moses
16. 3. 38

Dear Father Freud,

Today is not a nice day; there is a trough of low pressure and straightaway one gets a migraine and becomes irritable. My deputy-secretary has rung up to say she cannot come today and I myself am lacking in both zest and inspiration and nothing is going right. I spoke to Eitingon on Saturday and to S. yesterday; we would very much like to know whether the Princess or Dr. Jones has come. How will it now be possible for one of us to visit you and talk to you?[1]

At last I have finished my essay for *Imago* on 'A Peculiarity of the Ten Commandments'.[2] But I wrote it for a new American magazine and it is in too intimate a style for a review of the standing of *Imago*. I would have liked to change

---

[1] Hitler's entry into Vienna had taken place on 11. 3. 38.
[2] A. Zweig: '*Eine Besonderheit der zehn Gebote*'.

the style somewhat and put in a few quotations which had to be omitted for publication in America. But where will this recast essay now find *Imago*?

At the moment we have no real idea of how you are situated; are you still working? Or is the weather already warm enough for Anna to take you for drives in the car? That would be nice, for you must remember that without you we are like a flock without a shepherd, like children without a father, to put it in Biblical terms.

Recent developments in your country have naturally taken us by surprise; me less than the others. André Germain's essay was calculated to prepare us for much that has happened, but all the same our anxiety is naturally very great. The Berggasse dominates all our thoughts; we hope to get a few words from you soon.

And your family? Your wife, Anna, Martin, Tante Minna? Please give them best wishes from all of us. I in particular am looking at your photos, the most recent ones in the *Autobiography*,[1] and I imagine to myself that in your private world everything remains as we know and cherish it.

Your somewhat depressed

A. Z.

If you should have sent news to Eitingon and do not feel like writing any more, that will suffice for the time being as he will be kind enough to keep us informed.

Vienna IX, Berggasse 19
21. 3. 38

Dear Meister Arnold,

Since seeing your handwriting in this morning's (meagre) post, I have very much wanted to send our news so that you should not believe for a day longer than necessary that I am indifferent to your concern.

[1] S. Freud: *An Autobiographical Study* (1925). *St. Ed.* **XX**, pp. 7 ff.

I have just come through some particularly unpleasant weeks. Four months ago I had one of my normal operations, followed by unusually violent pain, so that I had to cancel my work for 12 days, and I lay with pain and hot-water bottles on the couch which is meant for others. Scarcely had I resumed work when these events occurred, world history in a teacup, which have changed our lives. On the wireless I was able to listen first to our challenge and then to our surrender, to the rejoicing and the counter-rejoicing. In the course of this 'eventful week'[1] the last of my few patients have left me. I am not yet quite free from pain, so I cannot work and therefore I do absolutely nothing. Our house is certainly very unsettled; friends come to enquire how we are; two very welcome guests, Princess Marie (Bonaparte) and Dr. Jones, have been constant visitors. They both came mainly to represent the international rights in the Verlag and the Institute. Jones left yesterday after he had conferred with Dr. Müller-Braunschweig of the German Psycho-Analytical Society, who had been summoned from Berlin. The princess, of inestimable value to us all, is still here. Unfortunately I am not the only invalid. Tante Minna is still in hospital after two operations for cataract. The operations went off well but her general condition is not satisfactory. My wife and two daughters are well and are coping efficiently, especially Anna. Since our usual move to Grinzing is now very unlikely we are giving much thought as to where we shall spend the spring and summer. We have not come to a decision yet. The time is not yet ripe for any change of habitat. It may take weeks before we decide.

Meanwhile please pass on the important items in this news, especially to Eitingon. I send my warmest greetings to you and to your wife and family – and with some confidence I trust I shall see you again this year.

Yours
Freud

[1] English in the original.

Vienna
21. 5. 1938

Letter received.[1] 39, Elsworthy Road, London N.W.3.
Uncertain when: we hope before the end of May!

Ever yours

Fr.

Haifa, Mt. Carmel
4. 6. 38

Dear Father Freud, dear Frau Professor, dear Anna,

Last night our faithful friend Eitingon rang up to say that
you all leave Vienna tomorrow morning. And although I
still cannot quite believe that everything will go according
to plan, I want to think that after all the frightful things
that have happened, this little favour of fortune will at last
come off. And so my congratulations and from the bottom
of my heart I wish the stupid old formula: Thank God!
Your card, dear Father Freud, came like a good omen,
though your handwriting revealed what your words had
perforce to conceal. But whatever may have been lost, whatever must be built anew, the main thing is: You are out and
you look back on the smoking ruins like people fleeing from
Sodom. . . . That it had to come to this, that the lords had to
hand over Vienna and Austria to these villains, to show in
what a world we live! How terrible, how tragic! And that
you should all have stayed on there, trusting in Schuschnigg,
till the rubble covered you like an avalanche! But now
everything will be better and easier and slowly peace and
joy in your grandchildren, of whom you have been deprived
for so long, will return to your wounded heart.

Did Martin cross the frontier illegally as we have been told?
Did he manage to save anything of the funds of the Verlag
or of your own money? How wisely you warned me in my
day. And yet only one thing is important: you breathe free

[1] Refers to an unpublished letter of Zweig's.

air and can once again look out of your window without looking on to the scum of human society.

A good rest, nothing but that for the present is my wish now for you all and especially for you yourself.

Yours
Zweig

Dita sends greetings, too, of course.

Vienna
4. 6. 1938

Leaving today for 39, Elsworthy Road, London N.W.3.

Affect. greetings[1]
Freud

Haifa
4. 6. 38

To Father Freud

What I was before I met thee
Lies now within these pages clear.
What life was blessed like thine so richly?
What knowledge had like thine such power?

A. Z.

Mt. Carmel
18. 6. 38

Dear Father Freud,

Receiving your two cards up here was like getting a touch from your hand. Fortunately we knew through the wireless and a telephone call from Eitingon that the most important thing had been achieved. You are now in safety,

---

[1] Original all in English.

no longer exposed to years of vindictive persecution. And even if your poor brave sister-in-law is still very ill, as St. Zweig wrote to me, a nightmare has passed from us all. You will have found my first letter to Elsworthy Road awaiting you on arrival. The newspapers have already answered many of our queries; your archives, your books, your collections have been saved. And Jofi, is she already . . . I have just noticed my strange mistake. I meant to ask about Lün. But a move like yours is after all a kind of resurrection, the journey like a voyage from the land of the dead, the incursion of the Egyptian darkness over Vienna like an onslaught of death. So Jofi might well reappear, mightn't she?

I think frequently of you, but at present more frequently of Anna. She, after all, has had to leave behind both her work and joy in the living Austrian reality. For the children she looked after as well as for Hochroterd there can be no substitute. Confound it all, that this should have come about because the cowardice of Schuschnigg could be exploited by the calculating military tactics of the English or by the shrewd capitalism of the high Tories around N. Chamberlain. One thing is certain: however much Lord Halifax tears his hair it will not help us; Vienna has gone. I hope to find a good description in Gibbon of the capture of Rome by the Goths, better still I would like to read (but where?) of the taking of Byzantium by Murat or of Jerusalem by the Crusaders.

But now you must rest. Your good wife will have a lot to do for her sister before she can relax. And when you feel you could and would like to see one of us I will come. My analysis with S. is approaching its end. Then I am going on a saltless diet for my eyes. But after that I could come to Europe. And Europe is now such a small place: France, Holland, England, Scandinavia, that is all. You know that Thomas Mann is staying on in the U.S.A. We have not decided what we will do next May, but we shall leave Palestine with heavy hearts. I cannot say much about that as yet. Our concern for the next few months will be how we are to reestablish your Verlag.

The *Einsetzung* appears to be getting a good press in England and America. But about sales the people are sceptical.

Meanwhile best wishes to you and to your successfully transplanted household.

Yours
Zweig

Haifa, Mt. Carmel
24. 6. 38

Dear Father Freud,

I have just heard with immense pleasure that they are once again bringing your name to the notice of the Nobel Committee. Modest though I am, I would like to point out that I exchanged letters with Th. Mann on this subject as long as two years ago. This time I do hope something will come of it. Otherwise it would be too ridiculous.

Today I have to write in this large hand as my reading eye is somewhat tired. The violence of the skunks in Berlin must be produced by some kind of inner pressure, or else they must be preparing to chuck out the 'grumblers' in case of war.

Here we are busy collecting secondhand analytic literature as printing copy for later.

Would it be possible for Anna, to whom I send my warmest greetings, to stamp and post the enclosed letter? Many thanks. I am always close to you in spirit.

Yours
Zweig

When we heard that you had had to give your collections voluntarily to the City of Vienna, Adam said immediately: 'Then we must send the Professor back straightaway the beautiful vase he gave me.' When I told him you might perhaps be hurt if he returned your present, he said in alarm: 'Then we'd better keep it.'

39, Elsworthy Road, London N.W.3
28. 6. 1938

Dear Meister Arnold,

Do not let yourself get worked up about the Nobel chimaera. It is only too certain that I shall not get the Prize. Analysis has several very good enemies among the personalities upon whom the award depends, and no one can expect me to hold out till they are either converted or have died out. So though the money would be very welcome after the way the Nazis bled me in Vienna and since neither my son nor my son-in-law is a rich man, Anna and I have agreed that one is not bound to have everything and so we have decided, I to renounce the Prize and she the journey to Stockholm to collect it.

Everything is going very well with us, or would be, if the distressing news from Vienna and the continuous appeals for help, which only serve to remind one of one's own helplessness, did not stifle every feeling of well-being. This is no topic for a short letter.

We posted your letter to the Home Office and though we were curious, we were decent enough not to open it.

I am enjoying writing the third part of *Moses*. Just half an hour ago the post brought me a letter from a young American Jew imploring me not to deprive our poor unhappy people of the one consolation remaining to them in their misery. The letter was friendly and well intentioned but what an overestimation! Can one really believe that my arid treatise would destroy the belief of a single person brought up by heredity and training in the faith, even if it were to come his way?

To come back to the Nobel Prize: it is scarcely likely that

official circles would decide to make as provocative a challenge to Nazi Germany as the awarding of the Prize to me would represent.

I have had several interesting visitors: Professor Yahuda, Prince Löwenstein, Wells ..., R. Bermann (Arn. Höllriegel[1]; do you know him?), Zweig, Prof. Malinowski,[2] and I am expecting others. What pleased me most was the visit of the two secretaries from the Royal Society who brought the sacred book of the Society for me to sign, since a fresh indisposition (bladder trouble) prevents me from going out. They left a facsimile of the book with me and if you were here I could show you the signatures, from I. Newton to Charles Darwin. Good company!

With warmest greetings to you and your wife and children,

Yours

Sigm. Freud

P.S. I have to accustom myself to a new signature since here, so they have instructed me, it is reserved for lords to sign with the surname only. Altogether a strange country.

Mt. Carmel
16. vii. 38

Dear Father Freud,

Your splendidly bright letter cheered me up so much that I wanted to answer it straightaway. I was just waiting for the arrival of the complete galley proofs of the little novel dating from my youth which I have touched up, so that I could tell you they were on their way to you. Then our friend Eitingon decided on his trip and I gave him the galleys (incomplete) together with a large photo of myself, so that I could appear alongside him at your house. But alas, the Unconscious or something prompted him to leave both photo and galleys behind in the Haifa Customs House, and

[1] Arnold Höllriegel: Austrian writer and journalist.
[2] Bronisław Kasper Malinowski (1884–1942): Anthropologist.

164

since we live de facto in a state of war, the port is hermetically sealed and we will have to wait and see if and when the photo and galleys are returned to me and then how they shall make their way to you.

And now yesterday a bomb was thrown into the Arab market place on a Friday, just when the streets were particularly full and the villagers from the surrounding country districts, who are in any case oppressed by terrorists, were doing their shopping. Since the whole country in its cowardly fear of Jewish nationalism has just made its obeisances to an eighteen-year-old assassin (who has unfortunately been hanged), there can be no doubt that this bomb was thrown by Jews. A terrible vengeance will descend upon us all. I only hope that we, my little family and I, will remain unscathed. But that is not certain. The Jews, who came to this country against the will of the Arab majority and who since 1919 have been incapable of winning the good will of the Arabs, had only one thing in their favour: their moral position, their passive endurance. Their aggression as immigrants and the aggression of the Arab terrorists cancelled each other out. But if they now throw bombs, I see a dark future ahead for us all. Until yesterday I was more or less unworried and I went about Haifa as I always have done. Now, however, I begin to feel threatened. Will we be able to stick to my programme and stay here till the end of April 1939? At any rate I am packing up my manuscripts and my winter clothes—and what was the first thing your admirer Adam said? 'And the Professor's books too.'

And when I objected that they were so heavy, he almost began to cry and said we could not leave these precious books behind and that there were only eleven or twelve volumes in any case. That I should leave my own books behind seemed quite right and proper to him, ungrateful child. (That is what we would have been called in a like case.) But you see from this that you are assured of the loyalty and gratitude of the next generation.

The letter, which I thank you very much for posting, was not to the Home Office but to the War Office. It contained some suggestions about experiments which might be undertaken to improve the shape of grenades; this would secure a higher trajectory and consequently a greater range and thus also an increased ballistic efficiency. If I come to Europe, i.e. to London, I will bring a memorandum on the subject with me. A large (and inexpensive) improvement in the artillery of both naval and military forces could be achieved – this way. But what is to happen if the authorities simply do not *want* to rearm adequately? I thought for a long time before deciding to send my opinions on this matter to the English rather than to the French War Office. But I am a Palestinian subject, so I really had no choice.

Yes, the English. But the individuals are charming. I would come to see you right away, Father Freud, but first of all I must scrape some money together. Lots of things have gone amiss for me this year. As early as February I began negotiations with American newspapers and I counted firmly on the New York Book Club. But it has all come to nothing. For two months we lived on our savings and now money is only just trickling in. In spite of all our economies our last trip cost us many, many pounds. But I am trying a few more things and then I hope I shall still be able to come to England by mid-August. Next year we want to emigrate from our poor Palestine and that will cost a mint of money.... Terrible that considerations like this should be our daily preoccupation in life.

Ah well, I will do all I can to make it feasible. Meanwhile I am looking forward to *Moses III*. As for myself, I am working at an essay on Spinoza[1] which you will enjoy. I get many contributions to American journals returned as being 'above the heads of our readers' and I am hatching new novels. As I walk past my volumes of Shakespeare, I wonder how your

[1] A. Zweig: *Spinoza, Presented by Arnold Zweig*. Longmans, Green & Co., New York, 1939.

vision of him is taking shape in London and whether you will choose Hobbes, who led a remarkable and very long life, as your patron saint.

Greetings to all and au revoir.

Yours
A. Z.

Mt. Carmel, Haifa, House Dr. Moses
5 Aug. 1938

Dear Father Freud,

The gods have given their sign: an unexpected cheque has arrived – from Russia, no further word as yet; and on the 18th I set off on the *André Lebon* for Marseilles and at the beginning of September I shall be with you and yours. Thank God.

Everything else can be arranged later. I have held back the copy of my new book. I wanted to write something in it specially for you and then get it sent off from Amsterdam. They sent me only two and a half copies here, and one I needed for the Spanish Relief Fund in Denmark and the half-copy (sheets, unbound) for corrections, misprints. But it has only been out a few days.

I hope you are not all suffering from the heat. Here on the mountain it is always bearable but humid, everything gets mouldy. Books on shelves have to be put out and aired in the sunlight, just like beds.

On the balcony next door a Jewish child is singing so out of tune that I had to stop writing because it was getting on my nerves like a gnat. He is singing the lechwod schabat song in honour of the Sabbath that is just starting. Then I remembered that in Berlin and Vienna and elsewhere Jewish children cannot sing any more, and so I refused to be put out. Tonight my Michi is going on guard duty, taking my little car with him. It is more a precautionary measure than anything else. Dita said to me just now: 'Time passes quickly. Scarcely have you got over the war when your son is doing guard duty.' Big wars always bring these secondary wars in their wake. History has other interesting parallels to this.

Dear Father Freud, I am so happy that I shall be seeing and talking to you soon. I have got my summer catarrh now, just as I had last year and the year before. I hope I shall have got rid of it before I sail.

With warmest greetings to your household from ours

Yours
Zweig

Warm greetings to Eitingon too. Perhaps I will enclose a few lines for him or write a separate letter tomorrow.

Sanary (Var)
25. 8. 38

Dear Father Freud,

I landed in Marseilles yesterday and radiantly happy I proclaim myself once more a European. In the Strait of Messina two journalists and I invested in a bottle of champagne to drink the health of the old Europe, to cry 'abasso!' and 'a morte!' to the dictators and at the same time to think of you: Thank God that you are out of it all. Now I must visit some friends here, meet various literary figures in the shape of Werfel, Ludwig Marcuse[1] and Schickele[2] and goodness knows who else. And at the beginning of the week I hasten on to Paris, spend three days there and then I shall be with you. I hope you are as well as last year. This time my throat is making only modest protests. At least I shall be able to talk with you. I think of spending three weeks in London and of opening up many practical projects if I

---

[1] Ludwig Marcuse: German writer.
[2] René Schickele (1883–1940): Alsatian novelist, dramatist, poet.

can. But for the moment I just send greetings to all your
family and especially to you.

Yours
Zweig

I have taken the liberty of getting my post forwarded to you.
I hope this will not be a nuisance. Did you get my Spinoza
essay all right? And would you be kind enough to save the
stamp on this letter for your special admirer, Adam? He
loves and honours you with the greatest devotion and
understanding, because the type of analysis we have carried
out with one another has helped him so much. Unfortunately
Eitingon had to hurry back home. I would like to have met
him in Paris.

Paris
16 Oct. 38

Dear Father Freud,

Before continents and oceans divide us once more, I must
thank you again and say au revoir. It was certainly exhausting for you and it was painful for me to appear in your
presence with my affairs in such disarray. But I have continued to try to make myself calmer and I shall go on trying.
I am so happy to have seen you established in your temporary
home with everything round you so bright and green. I am
happy too that you are able to go on working at your own
desk surrounded by your beautiful little gods,[1] employing
that indefatigable discernment which is your prerogative.
And to have seen you in the setting of your new home, with
your heart, your great silent love, your great silent suffering
for our wretchedly divided humanity. I am already looking
forward to seeing your garden when I return in the spring
or summer.

You have successfully interpreted and unravelled my
psychological make-up. But all the other elements within

[1] The reference here is to Freud's collection of antique statuettes.

me are still in a state of flux and prevent me from developing deeper ideas and making clearer decisions about life–how long will it be till I find the 'magic formula'? At any rate I am happy and grateful for the hours spent with you in what was a particularly dark time for you, and I sincerely hope that for you and yours the winter will be easier than was the early autumn.

Your faithful
Arnold Zweig

Haifa, Mt. Carmel, Beth Moses
8. xi. 38

Dear Father Freud,

It is now raining here with a savage violence; the roar of the breakers thunders up the mountainside as in R. L. Stevenson. Suddenly it has turned into winter. This increases the weight upon our hearts as it means that the time is physically as well as morally and politically dark. You can read and hear what is happening here on the wireless. What is happening in Europe is far more evil and unpleasant. I do not think these appeasers will understand what a price they are making others pay–till they have to pay it themselves.

Are you all right? Have you recovered from the great strain of the operation and its after-effects? Has some order been established in your household? I, at any rate, returned home deeply refreshed from my long stay in London and from being with you and talking with you; perhaps my pleasant sea trip also contributed to this. But now, faced with the task of either selling everything here or leaving it behind or giving it away, our furniture included, and setting off for America, my heart fails me. Freight charges are so high that we can only take suitcases and a few packing cases with us containing the most important books and our best gramophone records. This is all so symbolic and symptomatic that my arms just drop helpless to my sides.

Since I have been badly represented so far by both my publisher and agent, I must make new business contacts. *Versunkene Tage*[1] will not do by itself. But I have not got enough zest to write my boyhood novel. It seems meaningless to project further works of art upon this sinister background. It repels me so. I am afraid the machine age has resuscitated the insect soul within mankind and that the cultural attrition caused by the war has brought this to the surface. Ants and termites are getting ready to swamp the globe. Meanwhile the democracies are behaving like impotent parasites. Can one create works of art in such an atmosphere?

Warmest greetings, especially to your wife and Anna,

Yours gratefully

A. Z.

Poor fountain pen and no proper glasses for writing.

Assutah Private Hospital
Tel Aviv
5 Dec. 1938

Dear Father Freud,

These my first lines.[2] I am in bed. . . . Up for half an hour today for the first time. All well . . . my mental faculties . . . Most warmly of you and of Anna. . . .

A. Z.[3]

20, Maresfield Gardens, London N.W.3
13. xii. 38

Dear Meister Arnold,

Eitingon has been most kind in sending news about you but it is a different thing seeing your own handwriting again.

[1] A. Zweig: *Versunkene Tage*. Querido Verlag, Amsterdam, 1938.
[2] Arnold Zweig had been involved in a serious motor accident.
[3] Nothing further can be deciphered of this letter.

The good tidings one has counted on become all the more credible. The madness and senselessness of fate! And why must we be thus reminded of the uncertainty of our lives, of which we are in any case convinced. I was also very worried about your son who was driving the car—I thought it was Adam—because no mention had been made of him for such a long time. Glad to hear that he was absolutely blameless. May the devil not forget that drunken officer when he is choosing from among the English.

Not much to report from us. Everything would be fine were it not for this, that and the other. . . .

I am still waiting for a second sequestrum, which should come away like the first.

Please thank your wife for what she added to your letter and specially warm wishes for your speedy recovery.

Your old friend
Freud

Pension Käte Dan, Tel Aviv
17. 12. 38

Warmest greetings after my resurrection.

Yours
A. Z.

Carmel
29 Dec. 38

Dear Father Freud,

I have been home again since the 25th. I am still unsteady in my gait and giddy when I lie down or get up, and there are still some bruises which keep on reappearing. I am also very easily fatigued by people and so I have seen only very few as yet. But apart from that everything is over, not like an encounter with death which it might easily have been. For the moment I cannot and do not want to work; for the first time since the war I have a lot of leisure. I am also taking a rest from daily political life. And the thought often worries me that I taxed your strength unduly during my stay in London and bothered you with all too detailed narratives from the story of the two young treasure-seekers in the Zoo. I now think that I cannot write the book in this way; the German-Jewish St. Bartholomew's Night would have to be included too and that would necessitate many changes, large and small, in the plan. Perhaps this summer I will do the novel about 1914 (Title: '*Tis Now 25 Years Ago*), which would have to hint at consequences reaching up to the present day.

And how are you? I was pleased to hear from Eitingon what a wonderful recovery Fräulein Bernays has made – how good that is for her sake and your wife's! My wife has had her nerves taxed beyond endurance, but now she too is relaxing. A new epoch is dawning for her too and we are having a holiday together such as we have not had for a long time.

Heavenly weather à la niçoise changed into rain yesterday; soft, abundant rain, and winter is coming in. All the best to you, dear Father, and to Anna, Martin and all your household. Will 1939 unite us once again? Shall I not have to take my brave Michael over to the U.S.A.? All uncertain. Farewell to you in your beautiful study with the green lawn before your window; a happy New Year?

Your faithful
A. Z.

P.S. Your letter of 13. xii has just been forwarded here. Such delays occur often now. I do not know, of course, whether the army is to blame. But the driver of the tank behaved very well afterwards and helped Michi to get me out of the car. And my son – I am pleased you took his part so fervently – he behaved like a gallant son and comrade and it was just false rumours that fixed the blame on him. He is still in

Beirut with the car, getting it painted and having a holiday. I am grieved that all is not well with you.

You have had enough to bear in the year that is ending. All good wishes for the sequestrum and your progress. It was a joy to see your writing.

Yours
Zweig

Dita sends warmest greetings, Adam too. Did his letter of thanks ever reach you?

Mt. Carmel, House Moses
6. ii. 39

Dear Father Freud,

I am uneasy at not having heard from you for so long. I hope it only means that you are thinking of other things than me, and that you are well and of good heart and are working and thinking as ever. I wanted to be in Jerusalem on Saturday to get news of you. But my strength is still not up to it. My eye specialist and oculist are both in Tel Aviv and that was as far as I could manage. I spoke on the telephone with Eitingon and I hope to see him in about a fortnight.

All this time I have been more depressed than ever. My nerves are in a bad state. Both on the journey there and back I was afraid of being ambushed. This journey took place on the anniversary of my father's death, which made me apprehensive on Michi's account in view of the grandson-grandfather relationship—and he does in fact resemble his grandfather.

I am working at trifles, dealing with overdue correspondence, making plans for America. Am very unhappy at having to be homeless again. But what affects me most deeply is the public issue: Spain. The third victim after Austria and Czechoslovakia, and not the last. Yesterday our housekeeper's brother was shot dead in a bus here—he had been here only twelve days, after having escaped from Hitler. Ultimately it is only your work which explains what we are experiencing: civilisation's discontents are now coming to the surface. The peoples of the West are avenging themselves for centuries of repression. That is the only explanation of their frightful idiocy. I would like to write an essay on this subject soon.

We are all thinking of you, especially Adam and I.

Yours
Arnold Zweig

Versunkene Tage has still not found an Anglo-Saxon publisher.

20, Maresfield Gardens, London N.W.3
20. 2. 1939

Dear Meister Arnold,

Your letter has reminded me that you will soon be leaving the Unholy Land and its foothills, and so I must overcome my present disinclination and send you our news in writing. Unfortunately it is about my own state of health which threatens to become interesting. Since the operation in September I have been suffering from pain in the jaw, and this has increased slowly but steadily, so that without hot-water bottles and large doses of aspirin I would not get through my daily tasks or my nights. On an earlier occasion a fairly large sequestrum of bone was discharged; it was expected that this process would be repeated and settle the affair, but so far this has not happened. They are uncertain as to what is taking place and do not know whether the delay is basically innocuous or whether it is a further step in the mysterious process we have been combatting for sixteen years.

The very reliable doctor we have chosen here, Dr. Trotter, F.R.S., is against a further operation and recommends radium treatment, should any treatment prove necessary, but he cannot yet decide and confines himself to observation.

Princess Marie, who has spent the last few weeks with us, has got in touch with the Paris authority on radium treatment, since this treatment requires particular care and experience and there is no better man to be found anywhere. He is prepared to come to London and take over my case, but he stipulates that the diagnosis must first be established beyond all doubt. If Trotter decides to call him in, Anna and Dr. Schur and I would go over to Paris to stay for about four weeks in the hospital connected with the Radium Institute. But as yet I know nothing at all and can well imagine that the whole thing signifies the beginning of the end which always lies in wait for us. Meanwhile I have this paralysing pain.

Your depression is understandable enough, but it will certainly soon be overcome. Nothing serious has happened to you and I hope nothing will. I am not surprised that *Versunkene Tage* has not found a publisher. It is too innocently charming for this day and age.

I hope you will have no reason not to write to me, and I want to hear good news of you and yours.

With warmest wishes for your journey to remoter parts

Your faithful

Freud

Mt. Carmel
27 Feb. 39

Dear Father Freud,

It would have been wrong if you had concealed from me what you are having to endure once again. In spite of everything at this time I have felt deeply and happily immured in your atmosphere! For I have discovered, and derived a certain consolation from the discovery, that the explanation of the pile of ruins on which we and the dictators now live like rats, is to be found in your work—in your *Civilisation and its Discontents*. Your ideas alone explain the hatred and

176

indifference to everything that culture has achieved and signi-
fied since Moses. I intend to write an essay on this subject,
if you do not wish to do so yourself. Gentlemen are at last
able to shake murderers by the hand without falling into
disrepute. All ethical principles have been abrogated without the façade of law and order being demolished. What
more can Europeans ask? Will America be spared this plague?
What do you think about it? For us this question is not a
theoretical one. We must get away from here; we cannot
carry on financially any longer. It is an expensive country
and I am not earning anything here. I would prefer England,
on your account. But in view of the children's future and the
danger of war, America seems a wiser choice. I need a holiday
and a long sea voyage will be a kind of sanatorium for me.
Direct connection by sea; small, comfortable boats take
twenty-three days from Haifa to New York. From 3–26 April
I am supposed to be there for the P.E.N. Club Congress. To
see Roosevelt etc. My play *Sendung Semaels* is to be put on
over there. I shall try to get an immigration permit as a
tourist. I would like to get Michael into a technical school
there where he would be able to make his way and earn
something as well. He would like to become a pilot. He loves
engines and seems to have the soul of the engine in him.

Let us have the opportunity to follow the development of
your bone sequestrum. Could Anna relieve you of the bother
of writing, if it is a burden to you?

All good wishes to you, gallant pioneer.

Yours
Zweig

20, Maresfield Gardens, London N.W.3
5 March 1939

Dear Meister Arnold,
    In receipt of your letter of 27. 2, which gives me the dates
of your journey to New York (April 3–26. Is this definite?).

I think you are right to have chosen America instead of England. In most respects England is better, but it is very difficult to adapt oneself here and in any case you would not have my presence near you for much longer. America seems an Anti-Paradise to me, but it has so much space and so many possibilities and ultimately one does come to belong there. Einstein told a visitor recently that at first America seemed like a caricature of a country to him, but that now he feels quite at home there.

I cannot imagine what 'consoling explanations' you have discovered in my *Civilisation and its Discontents*. Nowadays this book has become very remote to me. I am only waiting for *Moses*, which is due to appear in March, and then I need not be interested in any book of mine again until my next reincarnation.

I have had some unpleasant weeks, not just being ill and in pain, but also complete indecision about the next steps to be taken. Operation and radium treatment (Paris) were finally abandoned and the external application of Roentgen ray was decided on; this is due to start tomorrow. (There is now no further doubt that I have a new recurrence of my dear old cancer with which I have been sharing my existence for sixteen years. At that time naturally no one could predict which of us would prove the stronger.)

I have received your sketch of a novel about Solomon. I will not disguise from you that I am not in agreement with your use of fairy-story motifs here. Even in the story of the liver sausage I found the incongruity disturbing. I would like to give you the reason for my objection but I am too weak to do so. You would be more successful analysing the character of a Nazi.

More news when I am sure of your address.

Ever yours
Freud

Dear Father Freud,

Your letter of the 6th found me in a state of deep depression.
We had just been to Jerusalem to say goodbye to Eitingon.
He means so much for us on the credit side in the Palestinian
scales! Altogether tearing ourselves away from here is frightful, specially for me. I have struck so many roots of friendship
here, even though we never seemed to strike economic ones.
The unknown would not alarm me at all if I could leave a
permanent home behind me here, to which we could return
as a matter of course. But to leave everything all over again,
to break it all up! We have had to do it so often already!
As a child from Glogau to Kattowitz, after the war from
Berlin to Starnberg, then back again to Berlin and then from
Eichkamp to Haifa by way of Sanary–and now westwards
once more. What do you say to this nomadic life against one's
will? Anyone who gets as much from his imagination as I do
could surely have stayed peacefully in one place, couldn't he?

You should describe your struggle with your 'dear cancer'
yourself. Indeed I know of no one adequate to deal with the
material of your life except you yourself. The postscripts etc.
you might leave to us, the reviewers of your memoirs.
Eitingon told me that there already is in existence a biography
of you by Sadgers[1] and an account of the whole sad story.
But I know no one who could describe your life and your
advance into forbidden territory as the author of *Moses* could
do it. I am delighted as I read it in the *N.T.B.*, where it has
appeared previous to publication. It revived in my memory
the two unforgettable gifts you and Anna made me in Vienna,
when you read the book aloud to me on two occasions, and
since then it has been an integral part of my mind and thought.
I am full of questions about yourself, but shame and modesty
have so far prevented me from expressing these questions and

[1] Evidently a mistake for the book by Fritz Wittels, *Sigmund Freud, der
Mann, die Lehre, die Schule*, 1924.

will no doubt always do so. The Steinach operation, the cancer operation, the years in hostile Vienna, your experiences with Jung, Stekel, Rank: these are all things about which I would like to hear more. The epic of your life! My thoughts circle round your existence as round that of a loved person, for that is what you are to me. In this way I shall take you with me to America. And after that, what then?

Ever, ever yours
Zweig

American Export Lines
On Board S.S. Excalibur
Marseilles
13 April 39

Dear Father Freud,

I think anxiously about you now that the ship has started to move and we are cut off from regular news of every kind. I would so like to have travelled via London but then I would have had to give up my journey altogether. It is only now that I am beginning to feel a bit more normal. Not until yesterday and the day before in Genoa did I dare to leave the ship, tended by Michi, who is a real man and a good and faithful son. After an hour and a half in the streets of the quiet town I was quite ready to return. But the severe angst, which cost me so much in self-control and which we and S. attacked in vain, has gone. It has left just one ghost of itself still active within me: anticipatory fear of America. But I have got a fortnight of relaxation ahead of me and I am relying on Neptune, the Poseidon of this ocean, who has been so incredibly kind to us and will, we hope, remain so.

My thoughts turn constantly towards you. Into my book *Aufmarsch der Jugend* I have put a doctor from Czernowitz, a Dr. Tennenbaum by name, who is passionately concerned with the causes of cancer and with carcinoma as such. He was crippled in both legs in the witch hunt for spies in

Munich in 1914 but he remains a doctor engaged in the fight against cancer. You shall hear more about all this later. I have not been able to decide on a subject yet. Please give my greetings to Anna and to your wife and to all your household and think sometimes of your

Arnold Zweig

Sanary (Var)
26. vii. 39

Dear Father Freud,

A few lines from the Princess reached me in the midst of my preparations for my departure: you are not well and she is going to see you. But I must go home. I cannot come to you, poor man that Hamlet is. But let me be with you in spirit, with the warmest feelings of gratitude for all you have done for us and for what you have taken upon yourself and with the ardent wish that at last things may go better with you. You have taken so much suffering upon yourself, you do not need any more torment. Now it is enough, and may a peaceful contemplation of your statues, of your thoughts and of your loved ones, take the place of pain. We all wish nothing more profoundly than that things may go well with you, just as you would have it.

In sincere friendship and devotion

Yours
Arnold Zweig

Mt. Carmel
8. 8. 39

Dear Father Freud,

I have been home a week now and I hasten to tell you in all happiness how deeply convinced and moved I was by your *Moses*. I read it on the voyage from Marseilles, and I think I shall always connect the breadth and calm of the sea with the breadth and calm of your vision of the early history of the Jews and of mankind.

We were very worried about you during these last few days, and our faithful Eitingon was ready to fly to London to see you. But in my heart of hearts I was unshaken. I saw you as I have seen you during all these recent months in spirit and in truth. And I saw that you would continue your battle with that cursed unknown thing, the disease X. For many reasons which I will not go into now, I was convinced of this. It is very early in the morning, and mist such as you get in the mountains is passing over Carmel, while out of it there rises the sound of the picks and hammers of Arab stone-breakers who are building a house on the slopes of the hill.

I will see to it that I write an article soon for the *Weltbühne* on *Moses*. I mean to do a lot of work as the English are going to pay very little compensation for my accident and since last October my income has been nil and my prospects, as far as my agent can see, are wretched. But I am quite cheerful.

I found my wife and Adam in the best of fettle. The boy is a special joy, full of physical and intellectual élan, very charming but at the same time full of mischief and healthy aggressiveness and completely at home with the car. Dita now drives very well, and from Michi we get letters of great candour and affection.

So I am embarking on a new period of work under good auspices. If and when we move from here depends on the results of this period. I am not in a position at present to contemplate the expense it would entail.

Meanwhile from the bottom of our hearts we send you our warmest greetings in love, admiration and gratitude.

Yours

Zweig

Pity that you could not quote my *Caliban* anywhere! One particular passage encourages me to make this slight reproach. As a punishment Adam is going to translate a review of *Moses* for you from the Hebrew newspaper *Agudath Jisrael,* which a friend purloined from a sanatorium and brought to us. It is incredibly impertinent and funny.

Haifa
9 Sept. 39

Dear Father Freud,

I am sad at not hearing from you, though I appreciate all the reasons for your silence. At the end of August and beginning of September I stayed with Eitingon, and we believed that there had been an improvement in your condition. We comforted ourselves with this thought and we laughed at the reception *Moses* had received among the Hebrews. I am still worried that in my last letter I said in fun that Adam was going to send a translation of the most impertinent and most stupid review of your book 'as a punishment'. One should not use such words even in fun to one who has been our help and salvation as you have been, and who now has to suffer so much. Before I fall asleep I often think of how nothing can be done to alleviate that cursed pain of yours. Then I grow angry that I did not become a doctor and that I do not understand anything about such matters.

I would have written before this but the censorship of all mail and the delay connected with sending letters written in German discourage me. Now it appears that England and France are exempt from this censorship and so I am going to risk it. But I am keeping back my essay on *Moses* till I have something more definite.

I refused to believe that we were going to have a war, a second world war, till the last minute. The monstrous stupidity of this régime is just not credible. Though I always remembered the bit in the Parsifal story according to which Amfortas' spear is the only means of healing the wound it has itself inflicted. A profound piece of early insight, I think. What is its origin? Our life goes on just as before and yours too presumably proceeds along its usual channels. But what about the younger generation? What is Martin doing? And how will Anna's work be affected? Excuse my pen, which has spattered ink, and give my greetings to all your household.

But to you, dear Father, my sincerest wishes that you may be able to hold out and endure till the fall of our enemies, the Huns or the Hitlerites.

Ever yours
A. Z.

INDEX OF WORKS

GENERAL INDEX